Would I? Would You?

Edited by DR. HENRY EINSPRUCH

THE LEWIS AND HARRIET LEDERER FOUNDATION
1503 East Baltimore Street, Baltimore, Maryland 21231

CONTENTS

Introduction

Since the beginning of time, every
thinking man, in the course of his years, has
stood at a fork in the road. Will he hold to
the familiar, comfortable, accepted way of life
in which he grew up; or will he follow the
dictates of his mind and heart, and venture
out into new paths?

Such a person has been called "a trail
blazer," "an adventurer," "a hero," and
sometimes "a dreamer," "an escapist," or
"a mercenary."

The stories contained in this collection
are true. Each person had a decision to
make. Would I? Would You?

The Editor

On the Bowery
of New York

By WILLARD PRICE

"Come on and serve God and then if He doesn't give you satisfaction, go back and serve the devil again. You can't lose."

The speaker is a little Russian Jew with iron-gray mustache, gold teeth, sparse hair, concerned horizontal wrinkles across his forehead, steel-rimmed spectacles settled down over his nose, and the most cheerful smile any face ever wore. He is known up and down the Bowery as "Joe, the Jew."

"I've seen the time when I didn't have the money to buy the steam off a frankfurter," says Joe.

Now, during the daytime, he conducts a fine laundry business among Broadway clients. But at night he is to be found on the East Side, helping down-and-outs.

"I make my money on Broadway and spend it on the Bowery," he explains.

During the twenty-seven years since he himself found the Messiah, he has won over eleven thousand others. Surely a good return on the original investment.

When Joe gets up on a platform and talks his cheerful philosophy, sings his home-made songs, and smiles his God-made grin, there is no resisting him. He is far from handsome,

JOE JUSTUS

and his singing voice sounds like the delivery of a load of coal. But no one cares about that—least of all Joe.

Nor are the songs he has written gems of poetic art. In Joe's Russia the Jews were not allowed to attend the public schools. They had to support their own schools, and that took money. Joe's parents couldn't afford it, so he didn't go.

A man once said, "Your songs are all right, Joe, but they're not dignified enough."

To which Joe replied, "If you come down to some meeting, you will see that my audience is not very dignified either."

Although uneducated, Joe is intelligent and keen. He understands human nature, and he knows the Bowery from hot dogs to whiskey, and from the Penny Arcade to the pawnshops. His songs hit his congregation of "bums" exactly where they live. Hear him as he sings, "The Bowery Boy."

"Did you say the world's against you,
    For they tell you you're too old,
    Down and out you walked the streets
    On many bitter winters cold.
    Broke, I go, while all around me
    There is wealth to overflow,
    What's the use of struggling longer,
    I'll throw up the sponge and go."

And then, just when he has every bleary wreck in the audience saying, "Yes, that's me," he swings, in an irresistible spirit of optimism, into this chorus:

"Don't lose hope and don't despair,
    There's a God for you to care.
    Don't sit down in gloom and fret
    While there's corn in Egypt yet.
    Don't look down in dark dismay,
    Fondling troubles all the day.
    Look for brighter days ahead,
    Jesus lives and loves you yet."

Joe has unshakable faith. One night he affirmed that he believed every word in the Bible. A German heckler said, "I suppose you think you know all there is in that Bible."

"No," replied Joe, "I'm no student; I have not studied it as I should like."

"And still you believe every word of it?"

"Yes, I believe every word of it."

"Well," said the heckler, "I'm a German and I'm proud of it, because Germans believe in being scientific. And if you don't know what's inside of that Bible, and yet you believe every word of it, all I want to say is that you're the biggest fool I ever saw." And he looked about for approval.

"Just one moment," said Joe. "You say you are a German?"

"Yes."

"Then I suppose you like frankfurters and sauerkraut?"

The German gave an affirmative grunt.

"Well, now listen, my dear German friend. Answer me this question: Have you ever studied the inside of a frankfurter?"

"No," growled the German.

"Well," smiled Joe, "if you have never studied the inside of a frankfurter and still you eat them, my dear friend, that's all I want to say to you."

Joe even gives the hecklers a chance. He tries to get his audience to talk. His own remarks and songs are brief, and his main effort is to induce the men to conduct their own meeting. He has even felt moved to write a few epigrams of advice. Here are some of them:

"Plenty of wind is a blessing to the windmill, but a calamity to a meeting."

"The fool has said in his heart, 'Lo, I am the anointed high-flyer in oratory.' The people said one to another, 'Behold a balloon filled with hot air.'"

"It is more blessed to give the rag to your neighbor than to chew it yourself."

As you walk along the Bowery with Joe, he is continually nodding here, throwing a word of greeting there, or stopping to speak with some friend. As you continue on, he tells you of the friend he has just met. This one used to be a professor. But he was so at odds with the universe that no college would keep him. He drifted down until he reached the Bowery, where Joe met him. Always complaining, he would rail volubly at the President and Congress, and if he had been Secretary of the Treasury, he would have sold government bonds in such and such a way. He could juggle millions, but then he would say, "Joe, can you lend me some money for a stew?"

Joe, untutored teacher, has taught the professor the lesson of Christian good cheer, and the professor has learned how to work at a job without complaining himself out of it.

Another friend, Joe tells you, once had a fine house and had made the first payment on the mortgage. But then he began to take too much liquid refreshment. He could not make the second payment, and the mortgage was foreclosed. He speedily drank himself down and out. One night he sat on the curb, a bleary red-nosed sot. Someone had given him a quarter and he was trying to decide whether to spend it on more whiskey or a bed. He decided on the whiskey, but before he could get to a dive, Joe caught him. The result was that a sister in a suburb received a request for a check which was spent on a new suit of clothes. With a bath, shave and haircut, a new suit of clothes, and an inoculation of Joe's hopeful Christianity, this man presented himself at his former office, got his job back, and has kept straight ever since.

But one of the most interesting stories I heard is the story of Joe himself as he told it while we walked up the Bowery late one night. Here is the story:

"Well, an anarchistic parade chased me into Christianity. Emma Goldman and Alexander Berkman held a parade and a meeting on Union Square. They railed much against the Government. It sounded very good to me for I had had nothing but bad luck since I came from Russia. I was dissatisfied. I was filled with sympathy as I listened.

"Then the police came. They broke up the meeting, clubbing everybody. They arrested the two speakers. I ran for sweet life. I kept on going down toward the Bowery, believing there was someone chasing me. Then, just when I thought I was safe, somebody grabbed my arm and I said to myself, 'Now for a night in the cooler!' But it wasn't a policeman. The man said, 'Come in!' I heard music and thought it was a place of amusement, so I said, 'I have no money.' The man said, 'You don't need money,' and took me inside. It was a Gospel meeting.

"That was my first contact with Christianity. Being a Jew, everything in me revolted against Christ and Christianity.

"But, from curiosity, I went again and again. I struggled not to go, but a power I could not explain drew me there time and time again.

"That was when I had a partnership in booze with an Irishman. I got a job in a pie factory in Brooklyn and in my spare time I would take my friend around to different saloons and treat him. It was a great combination. The Jew furnished the money and the Irishman furnished the thirst. Every night we got full of booze and frankfurters and he would 'carry the banner' (spend the night walking aimlessly up and down the Bowery), but I would go to the Gospel meeting.

"Four times I broke up the meeting. I would argue with the speaker. I always tried to fight off the influence by protesting. The last time they took me by the collar and said, 'You get out, and don't come back again.'

"As I went out I saw the sign over the door, 'God bless you, come again.' So the next night I came again.

"I used to sit there half dozing. One night a man got up and said, 'What shall it profit a man . . . ' When I heard that I woke up. You can't expect a Jew to sleep when he hears of profit!

"The leader of the meeting that night was a lady and she stood on the platform and said, 'Salvation for the drunkard!

Salvation for the gambler! Salvation for the thief! Salvation for the drug fiend! Salvation for everybody!'

"Then she looked at me and said, 'Salvation for the Jew!'

"At the invitation I went forward and gave my heart to God. I made a covenant to serve him if he would make a man out of me. God kept his part of the bargain and I'll try to keep mine.

"I cleaned up, bought a boiled shirt and collar, moved away from the Bowery to a furnished room, and got a job dishwashing in a restaurant. I saved up $40.00 and went in business for myself, lost my money and got married!

"On my wedding day my wife didn't have fifty cents and I didn't either. We got married on faith. Somebody gave us six teaspoons and an old stove.

"It was March and pretty cold. We had three rooms and a store, and one stove to heat them all. In the morning I would make fire in the store, and in the evening, when we wanted to retire, I would carry the red-hot stove, pipes and all, back into the bedroom. In the morning we started all over again.

"In the daytime I went around with a bag on my back soliciting laundry, and at night I worked.

"Today I have a steam plant of my own, the Joseph Justice Laundry. I've a good business on Broadway. People call me on the telephone and say, 'Joe come here,' and 'Joe come there.' I don't need to look for work, it comes to me.

"Salvation paid. I bring him misery; he gives me joy. I bring poverty; he gives me prosperity. I bring selfishness; he gives the joy of doing something for the other fellow. That is a good bargain. Salvation is a paying business. The proof of its being good is that a Jew has stuck to it for twenty-seven years."

While Joe had been telling his story, I had been watching the street we were following. It was very evident to me that if ever the humble ambassadors of faith, hope, and love, like Joe the Jew, were needed on the Bowery, they are needed now.

The Truth
About the Rabbi

By NAHUM BRODT

Max Wertheimer was born of Orthodox Jewish parents in Kippenheim, Baden, Germany. His earliest childhood recollection was of his parents rising very early in the morning in order to read the Hebrew Prayer Book, even in winter before the fires were kindled. They were devout and God-fearing.

At an early age Max was sent to *Cheder*, where for nearly ten years he was instructed in Orthodox Judaism. He was taught Hebrew; the five books of Moses; the *Pirke Avoth*, the ethics of the fathers which is a treatise of the Mishnah. He later went to *Gymnasium* for his classical studies, after which he was apprenticed to a manufacturer.

It was soon apparent that young Wertheimer was not suited to the business world, and since an injury received in early childhood left him with impaired health, his parents sent him to America for further education. It was their desire that he should study for the rabbinate.

At that time there were two rabbinical seminaries in the United States. The one in New York City was Orthodox in teaching, and the one in Cincinnati, Ohio, was Reform or liberal. Max Wertheimer had been in correspondence with

Hebrew Union College.

➤➤➤➤✺❖✺❖❖

Catalog and Program

OF THE THREE DEPARTMENTS:

Preparatory ❖ Rabbinical ❖ Semitic,

... 1899 - 1900 ...

'93 Rabbi Abraham Simon, B. A., Omaha, Neb.

'94 Rabbi George J. Solomon, B. A., Vicksburg, Miss.

'93 Rabbi M. G. Solomon, B. L.

'84 Rabbi Joseph Stolz, D. D., Chicago, Ill.

'89 Rabbi Max Wertheimer, Ph. D.

'98 Rabbi Harry Weiss, B. A., Pueblo, Col.

'98 Rabbi Philip Wolf, B. A.

'99 Rabbi Louis Wolsey, B. A., Little Rock, Ark.

'99 Rabbi Martin Zielonka, B. A., Waco, Texas.

CINCINNATI,

COLLEGE BUILDING, 720 W. SIXTH STREET.

Rabbi Isaac M. Wise, president of the Hebrew Union College of Cincinnati, with the result that he chose the Reform Seminary. This was a source of deep grief to his Orthodox parents who considered the Reform teaching of Judaism the equivalent of modernism.

The rabbinical course lasted eight years, but due to previous work, Max completed the prescribed studies in seven years. Upon graduation he became Rabbi of B'nai Yeshurun Synagogue, Dayton, Ohio, where he served with marked success for ten years, esteemed and loved by all.

When Wertheimer graduated in 1889, he received not only a degree of Bachelor of Hebrew Literature, but also a Ph.D. from the University of Cincinnati. His name is listed as an alumnus of Hebrew Union College, and, in fact, his is the only Ph.D. in the Catalogue and Program of 1897-1898, as well as in that of 1899-1900. From then on his name was dropped from the roll of graduates.

What happened?

In the NATIONAL JEWISH POST of November 25, 1955, Alfred A. Isaacs refers to Max Wertheimer as a graduate of Hebrew Union College who was disowned by his Alma Mater for the sole reason that he became a Christian.

It is generally assumed that a Jew becomes a Christian because he has been offered a job paying a fabulous sum of money. But let it be said—and this for the record—that as Rabbi of B'nai Yeshurun Synagogue, Dr. Wertheimer received a salary of $2,000 a year, plus house, fees from weddings, bar mitzvahs, and the like. When he became a believer in the Messiahship of Jesus he went back to school, after which he became pastor of the First Baptist Church, Ada, Ohio. What salary did he then get? The magnificent sum of $500 a year!

Thus it could not have been money which attracted Dr. Wertheimer. He was convinced, after much study and soul searching, that the messianic predictions in the Hebrew Bible found their fulfillment in him of whom Moses and the prophets wrote, Jesus of Nazareth, the Messiah of Israel.

A Trail Blazer
of Afghanistan

By LAURA WADE RICE

The stillness of midnight was broken by the sharp report of a pistol. The gray dawn revealed a lifeless body within the Mission compound.

Isidor Loewenthal was scarcely thirty-seven, his tenure of service in the East had not extended beyond nine years, yet he has been called "one of the most remarkable men that India has ever known."

Felled in his own garden by a shot from the pistol of his own Sikh watchman, strongly under Mohammedan influence, Isidor Loewenthal's dreams of winning Afghanistan for his Master seemed at an end. But seeming is not always being. Death itself cannot write finis to such a life or to such a lifework as his.

They bore him back to his room, a student's room, lined with books from floor to ceiling; books in many languages, rare copies, as well as the most priceless collection of ancient manuscripts to be found in any private library in India. On his desk lay the nearly completed manuscript of his Pushtu dictionary, copies of his other works in that language, and, superseding all, his crowning gift to the people of the Afghan-land, the New Testament in Pushtu, the common language of its millions.

Isidor Loewenthal

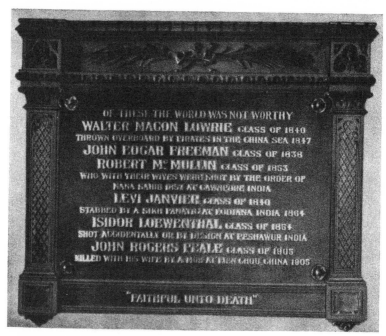

OF THESE THE WORLD WAS NOT WORTHY
WALTER MACON LOWRIE CLASS OF 1840
THROWN OVERBOARD BY PIRATES IN THE CHINA SEA 1847
JOHN EDGAR FREEMAN CLASS OF 1838
ROBERT McMULLIN CLASS OF 1853
WHO WITH THEIR WIVES WERE SHOT BY THE ORDER OF
NANA SAHIB 1857 AT CAWNPORE INDIA
LEVI JANVIER CLASS OF 1840
STABBED BY A SIKH FANATIC AT LODIANA INDIA 1864
ISIDOR LOEWENTHAL CLASS OF 1854
SHOT ACCIDENTALLY OR BY DESIGN AT PESHAWUR INDIA
JOHN ROGERS PEALE CLASS OF 1905
KILLED WITH HIS WIFE BY A MOB AT LIEN CHOU CHINA 1905

"FAITHFUL UNTO DEATH"

Memorial Tablet, Stuart Hall,
Princeton Theological Seminary

Though he had lived less than a decade in the East, men of the highest rank in civil and military life had come to Loewenthal for counsel and friendship. Few knew better than he the manners and customs of the people of the land, or were more familiar with Oriental politics. Socially he was a delightful member of any circle. Genius was his in the rarest sense. He was an accomplished musician, mathematician, metaphysician, and pre-eminently a linguist. As a philologist he stood in the front rank. His fine mind penetrated the intricacies of the religions of the East, and as a disputant with those who professed them, whether Mohammedan, Brahmin or Buddhist, he was always the master. As a Christian, he was sincere, humble, devout, and zealous.

The lips, now silent, had given God's message in many languages other than his own: Pushtu, Hindustani, Persian, Cashmere, Arabic, dialects of northern India, Hebrew, English, German, French. The heart, now still, had known tragedy and pain. Parents had spurned him and family position had been denied him when he chose Jesus as his Messiah.

It is a far cry from the grave under Eastern skies to Posen, Prussian Poland, and the Orthodox Jewish home into which Isidor Loewenthal was born. Graduating from the *Gymnasium*, where he studied the ancient classics, natural science, metaphysics, mathematics, music, Hebrew, and several modern languages, his father willed that he enter business. Isidor regretfully obeyed, but showed little aptitude for it. All his leisure hours were spent with his beloved books, so arrangements were made for him to enter one of the German universities. It was then that an event occurred that changed the whole course of his life and made him an exile from his native land.

Political dissatisfaction ran riot just then among German students. Young Loewenthal brilliantly set forth the spirit of the times in a satirical poem which found its way into one of the public journals. It was traced to him. Finding that he was in danger of arrest, he made a hasty escape via Hamburg to America.

In this strange land, almost destitute of means and ignorant of the English language, Isidor found life exceedingly hard. One by one his dream bubbles burst. Great New York had no need of him. Philadelphia opened no door to him. Perhaps he could find employment in the country. He trekked wearily from farm to farm, ready to exchange work for shelter, food, and a little money.

The sturdy farmers, glancing at his small stature, and learning that he knew nothing of farm work, did not hesitate to say no. Questions battled in his brain. What should he try next? Where should he turn? Had the world no need of him? What puzzling hand was shaping his destiny?

Heavy-hearted, he stooped to lift the burden exile had forced upon his people and became a peddler. With a basket stocked with thread, needles, buttons and other small articles, he began his weary tramp from door to door. He found little cash and less encouragement awaiting him, until one rainy night the dim lights of Rockland, a little town near Wilmington, Delaware, showed scattered doorways at which he knocked and solicited purchasers.

At length he reached the door through which he was to enter upon a new life. A motherly-faced matron asked him to come in while she looked over his wares. Completing his sale, he covered his basket to protect it from the rain and turned wearily to face the darkness and pitiless storm.

And then down the stairs came the man who was to have the most decisive influence on his life.

"Wait," said a kind, fatherly voice, "come in, get dry and warm, and stay and eat with us. It's a terrible night."

The forlorn, rain-drenched figure went to the speaker's heart. Talking later beside the fire, the Rev. S. M. Gayley, pastor of the Rockland Presbyterian Church, was amazed to find that his guest possessed more than ordinary education and was an accomplished linguist.

"You mustn't go out into the storm tonight. We have a spare bed. Tomorrow I'll try to find something better for you t'.in this sort of uncertain work."

Next morning, as his new-found friends knelt in family devotions, he courteously bowed with them and heard for the first time a Christian prayer. The Rev. Mr. Gayley soon found for him a position as teacher of French and German in Lafayette College, but he was invited to think of and use their house as his home. Isidor gratefully accepted their kindness.

Whether or not his benefactor guessed his race, Loewenthal did not know. No word of personal religious approach was made during his stay, but the atmosphere of the home, the intimate relationship with God that breathed in its daily devotions, required some explanation to the keen mind of the young man. Secretly he began to study the New Testament. Openly he sought to master English, often spending the whole night in study.

Tall, swarthy and intelligent, a new friend came into Loewenthal's life at Lafayette. His roommate was Victor Herschell, a Jew, but a Jew eager to serve the Christ whose Messiahship he avowed. Both were well versed in the Talmud, and the passing of the midnight hours concerned them little as they discussed the claims of Christ. Herschell's faith and life were, however, his most impressive argument. Loewenthal might discount Mr. Gayley, for was he not a Gentile and a Christian minister besides, but what was he to make of Herschell, cultured, refined, a man of his own race?

After a prolonged inward struggle, Loewenthal made a public profession of his faith and was received into the Rockland Church of which his friend was the minister. He continued to teach and to pursue his philological studies until he decided to enter the Theological Seminary at Princeton, N. J. He was graduated with the highest honors, and was elected essayist of the *Society of Inquiry* at the Commencement exercises. His masterly presentation of "India as a Field of

Labor'' showed great ability and a comprehensive knowledge of the subject.

He tutored for a while in Princeton College, during which time flattering calls came to the young Jewish Christian theologian to fill pulpits in established fields. But the longing of his soul was to carry the story of his Messiah to men who knew him not. He was licensed to preach by the Presbytery of New Brunswick, and later ordained as a missionary to India by the Board of Foreign Missions of the Presbyterian Church. Soon thereafter he set sail for India.

Before going to tell the story of his Messiah in a faraway land, he determined to make a personal effort to inspire his own family with the love that was now his dearest treasure. He had not heard from them since he wrote to them of Christ. Perhaps they would listen if he saw them face to face. And so, on his way to India, Isidor decided to stop off. He travelled to the old, well-remembered and dearly-loved home. But in vain. His parents refused to see him, but conscious of the presence of his Master, Isidor Loewenthal continued on his way.

Arriving at Rawal Pindi, north of Lahore, his first task was to begin a study of the necessary language. But which language? Three faced him: Hindustani, used by officialdom; Persian, spoken by the aristocracy; and Pushtu, the common language of Afghanistan.

Loewenthal determined to master them all, and add Arabic for religious discussions with Mohammedans. Easier far to scale the Suleiman mountains, which barred his way into the interior, than to conquer the intricacies of the language of the Afghans. But Loewenthal's indomitable will and his linguistically constructed brain set out to blaze a trail into the hearts of the people. At the end of the year he was sent to Peshawar, a city on the borders of Afghanistan.

"Peshawar," wrote Loewenthal after a short stay in the city, "is the Gibraltar of the East, where Jew and Gentile, exiled Europeans and refugee Asiatics, Bengalis and cutthroat Afghans meet and jostle one another. The people are the most turbulent, fanatical, and bigoted of all the peoples in India. The surrounding scenery is full of grandeur. Rising above all is the snow-capped peak of Takht-i-Suleiman, or 'Solomon's Throne.' "

How he longed to cross the Indus river and be one of the first to announce the glad tidings of salvation to the remote border of that forbidden land!

While he waited for a way of entrance to open, he spent his time in studying, preaching to the people, and, above all, in preparing a translation of the New Testament into Pushtu, the language of the Afghans. Without grammar or dictionary, the man to whom philology was a passion, set to work to ferret out meanings and constructions, significances and idioms; to talk over his conclusions with the most learned; to test out on the ignorant the clarity of his renderings; and to polish, revise, and perfect, in order that "the Word of God might have free course and be glorified."

Loewenthal felt that a good text of the New Testament was imperative as he was under command not to cross the border to preach, since insurrections were always seeking excuse to break out. Yet to the villages on the India side came Afghans from the interior: traders, learned Mullahs, zealous Imams, respectable Khans, who often carried home with them Loewenthal's Gift of Gifts, the story of Jesus in their own language.

One day we see him in the shade of a mosque, the fierce sun piercing even its shadow, and a group of Afghans pressing close to him. Gaily attired, each man carried a weapon. Their faces fierce and sensual, the name of Allah constantly on their lips, Isidor was "one against a thousand." What could he hope to do? Yet the fire of conquest for Christ that burned in Loewenthal's breast sent him everywhere he was permitted to go, to sow the seed of His story.

Strangely enough, these fanatics seemed eager to listen. Their mullahs, numerous as the priests of Baal against Elijah, lingered to debate, to pit their religion against his. Seemingly fruitless debates, yet they won him respect and friendliness.

"I find it impossible to get back from the preaching in the villages without being exposed to the sun longer than I can bear it, and the result is prostration," he wrote. "It is not so much the pain that I regret, as the absolute loss of so much time. In the evening there is a steaming crowd in the close bazaar with the thermometer near a hundred and not a breath of air. There is loud clamoring until the voice absolutely seems to refuse to sound."

Counting not his life dear for the sake of the Messiah he loved, Loewenthal pressed ahead along the path of steadily growing influence. Perhaps some day the ban would be lifted and he might pass into the land of his dreams.

Then, just when he began to sense possibilities of its coming, at an unexpected turn of the road, directly athwart his pathway, there stretched the measured length of an open grave.

*   *   *

"For the evangelization of the Mohammedan world," wrote Samuel Zwemer, in ISLAM, A CHALLENGE TO FAITH, "We need first and most of all, men—the best men. We need men who, in the spirit of Isidor Loewenthal, hold not their lives dear; men who carry the burden of these millions of Moslems upon their hearts, and, with Abraham of old, cry out: 'O that Ishmael might live before thee.' "

Abreast the heroes of Mohammedan missions stands Isidor Loewenthal, the raven-haired, black-eyed Jewish peddler, ambassador of Jesus the Messiah to far-off Afghanistan. Who doubts but that when they laid his body to rest, the soul of the man, stalwart, strong, and brave, went marching on with his Commander and Messiah into the forbidden land along the trail he had blazed for those who might come after him.

Such lives cannot die!

On the Wings
of Song

By SAMUEL GROSS

Felix Mendelssohn Bartholdy was born in Hamburg, the grandson of the great Moses Mendelssohn, philosopher, Jewish reformer, and intimate associate of Lessing, Herder and Kant. He was born amid refining influences, familiar with living poets, scholars and philosophers who frequented his father's house. At the age of eleven he met the poet Goethe, who was most impressed with "this wonderful grandson of Moses Mendelssohn who early showed gifts equal to Mozart's."

When Felix was seven years old his formal education began. Lessons included piano, violin, bass, counterpoint, and languages. By the time he was eleven he spoke French and English fluently, wrote a letter in good Italian, translated the "Andrea" of Terrance into German verse, and made good headway in Greek. He could ride, swim and dance, but was not fond of mathematics.

In his twelfth year he began to compose regularly, and before he was eighteen had completed twelve symphonies for strings, several songs, four organ sonatas, a cantata, and the score of the two-act opera, "Camacho's Wedding," from Don Quixote. He astonished the world as a full-fledged composer, a master of original imaginative genius, with the overture to "A Midsummer Night's Dream."

FROM THE ORATORIO ST. PAUL

At the age of twenty-eight Mendelssohn gave to the world the oratorio "St. Paul," and nine years later produced his masterpiece, the most popular of oratorios, "Elijah." Among his many compositions, "Songs Without Words," is perhaps the most admired, and who is not familiar with his "Wedding March" which invariably ushers in the bride!

He loved the organ, and was one of the most masterly organists and composers of his time. For intrinsic worth and beauty, his "Organ Sonatas" rank next only to those of Bach and Handel. He was musically and spiritually a true child of Sebastian Bach.

Hearing a complaint that Bach's music sounded like a mathematical exercise, Mendelssohn formed a choir of sixteen voices for the practice of the Passion Music. So great was the response to the heavenly music, that there was a demand for a public performance. Under the direction of young Mendelssohn, who conducted without notes, knowing the music by heart, the three to four hundred voices of the *Singakademie* overcame the intrinsic difficulty of the music. Leading opera singers undertook the arias, and with the aid of his actor-friend, Devrient, the performance was a success. A thousand people were turned away from the doors, and Mendelssohn later commented: "It was an actor and a Jew who restored this great Christian work to the people." That was the dawn of the Bach culture, and it was through Mendelssohn that Bach gained a foothold in the modern world of music.

Felix Mendelssohn, like his father before him, was identified with the Christian Church, but carried his Jewish heritage with great distinction. The Jewishness of his music is dealt with at length in Marco Rothmüller's study on THE MUSIC OF THE JEWS. He quotes Max Brod, author and composer: "Outstanding among Mendelssohn's works is his violin concerto which, by its profound passion, belongs among his most moving and beautiful creations. And it is just in this concerto that the Jewish note—albeit unconsciously used—can most clearly be heard, pervading the essence of the work rather than its details."

In some of his oratorios, with all the Jewish masculinity of his psalms, his male choruses, and his part-songs, the sentimental minor vein is dominant throughout the whole.

Many of Mendelssohn's melodies were accepted by Central European Jewry, which considered them Jewish in content, and used them either as instrumental works, or in arrangements adapted to the singing of various prayers in the synagogue.

Grove's DICTIONARY OF MUSIC AND MUSICIANS has this to say about the great composer: "It is generally noted that Mendelssohn possessed charm of manner to a high degree. For this, and for his business acumen, his appreciation of domestic propriety, his punctuality, his sense of religious duty, and a somewhat moralizing attitude, he was indebted to his upbringing and to the ancient traditions of his Jewish race. He had a markedly Jewish appearance."

The life of Felix Mendelssohn, though of short duration—less than thirty-nine years—was one of incessant activity. There is no question but that both his talents and the character of his compositions were largely the product of his heredity and environment.

Mendelssohn stands as the best modern representative of sound, many-sided, conservative, and yet progressive musical culture. He was an artist to the marrow, gifted with original creative genius. Of his complete musicianship there is no question. As performing artist, conductor, composer, he ranks with the greats. He was indeed a noble son of Israel, a Jewish Christian, whose life and work have greatly enriched the world.

The Love

That Did Not Fail

By ELINOR STAFFORD MILLAR

Few people have so touched my life as has a young Jewess of my country, Australia. Caroline Jonas was born into an Orthodox Jewish home, and a few incidents which she related to me will convey an idea of the atmosphere in which she grew up.

"My father insisted on his children going regularly to synagogue. One day, while yet a child, I said:

" 'Father, I do not feel any better from hearing the Rabbi. He talks Hebrew and I do not understand what he says. Will you please excuse me from going?'

"He answered, 'No, I cannot have a heathen in my family. I cannot excuse you. You must go.'

"We women and girls sat in the back of the synagogue, while the men worshipped on the floor in front. We sometimes discussed irrelevant matters—our servants, our engagements, the love affairs of our friends. Sometimes the women talked so loud that someone would shout:

" 'Will the women please keep silence in the synagogue!'

"I remember a yearly ceremony in our home—the celebration of the Passover. Two large cups were filled with wine. One was taken by the head of the house who pronounced a blessing upon it. Then he handed the cup to all the others

CAROLINE JONAS

who drank of it. The second cup of wine was 'Elijah's Cup.' Then the door of the room in which we sat was opened by the youngest member of the family. A solemn pause ensued. It is expected that at this moment Elijah will come and announce the glad tidings that Messiah is at hand. I was young and fearful, yet I was anxious, hoping and longing that perhaps he would come. Though I knew that for many years we had been expecting his arrival, yet I shall never forget the beating of my heart as the door was opened and we stood waiting for Elijah to come in and say, 'The Messiah is at hand!' "

When Caroline Jonas was eighteen or nineteen years of age, she was introduced into the best social circles of New South Wales. In speaking to me of this time of her life, she said:

"I was the daughter of rich parents. I had received a good education. I was attractive. My mother said to me, 'My dear, I expect you to make an elegant match, I expect you to marry some rich and prominent young Jewish man.' "

Imagine the horror and humiliation of her mother when Caroline confided to her that she had given her heart to a Christian! To her he was a Christian, inasmuch as he was not a Jew.

The mother said, "I cannot announce this. I must ask you to give me your word that you will never see this young man again."

Caroline was locked behind her own door. Needless to say, messages of love went both in and out of that room.

Later the mother, relenting somewhat, said:

"I will grant you as much as this: You may correspond with your friend, but I ask you to promise me that you will never marry him without my consent."

The daughter agreed. The mother kept the lovers apart for several years, but Caroline was unwavering in her love. She idolized the young man to whom she had given her heart. Finally the mother had a talk with her.

"I see you do not mean to change your mind. I must be considerate of you, for after all you are my daughter. If you are not going to marry any one else, but are determined to ruin your life, the time has come when I must yield to your wishes. If you still care to do so, you may write to your lover to come, and I will meet him."

Caroline said, "I sent one word, 'Come!'"

And he came. They walked together that afternoon, and were to return to dinner that evening.

What they said I do not know, but Caroline returned home alone. During the course of their conversation she learned that he had not been as true to her as she had been to him, and her proud heart rose in rebellion at his unfaithfulness. She turned him away with indignation. When she reached home her mother looked into her white face and asked:

"What happened? Where is your friend?"

The girl did not answer, but fainted away. She was carried to her room, and for months lingered between life and death.

Finally, when she was convalescent, she was sent to St. Kilda, Melbourne. She walked up and down the seashore, heart-broken, feeling that her loss was irreparable. One afternoon, as she looked out into the blue ocean, she said in her heart:

"I do not want to live, and tonight I shall end it all."

Caroline went back to the hotel, and as she walked up the broad stairway, she sighed heavily. A young woman going down the stairs heard her and said:

"Excuse me. You sighed deeply. Are you in trouble?"

Caroline replied, "Yes. I was thinking that life is not worth living."

"Indeed," said the young woman, "I think life is worth living."

Caroline turned with a little bow, a look of unbelief on her face, and said, "Your secret?"

The young woman replied, "My secret is that I have a Friend who comforts me in all my sorrows and delivers me out of all my troubles. He is my companion through life."

"I wish I had such a friend."

"You may have," the other reassured her. "I'd be glad to have you read the story of my Friend."

"A story?" queried Caroline.

"Yes," and saying this she drew from her bag a little leather-bound book. Caroline looked at it critically and slowly read the title, "The New Testament."

"Why, I've never seen this before. What is this book?"

"It's about my Friend. Won't you read it?"

Caroline shrugged her shoulders.

However, after a moment's hesitation, she took it and went on to her room.

What followed I give in her own words:

"I opened the book at the first chapter and read, 'The book of the generation of Jesus Christ, the son of David, the son of Abraham.' Something struck my heart, and I was almost afraid to proceed. But there was a fascination about the whole genealogy, and not one name did I miss.

"When further on in the same chapter I read, 'And thou shalt call his name Jesus, for he shall save his people from their sins,' I asked myself, 'Is this the one she meant? Is this the friend she spoke of who comforts her in her sorrows?'

"I was now much agitated, for was that not the name that was never allowed to pass my lips? But I read on, and the words burned like fire in my heart.

"When I came to the Sermon on the Mount, 'Blessed are the pure in heart; for they shall see God,' I thought, Why, nobody but a good man could ever say that! 'Blessed are they that mourn; for they shall be comforted.' My own heart was full of anxious care, sorrow, disappointment, and I wanted to draw near to him.

"Surely he is not the one whose name I was not allowed to utter, for he must have been good! Surely he is not the one for whom we are looking! If he is, how wonderful, and yet how terrible that we rejected him. And then I went so far as to say, 'God forgive me, but I half believe the story.'

"I read on to where he cleansed the leper, and gave new life and gladness and song to those who were in sorrow; to where he ate with publicans and sinners; and my heart was beginning to love him. And when he took the little children in his arms and blessed them, I said, 'I believe I love him.'

"I hurried on through the pages. I saw that I was letting my heart go out to him. Then I again asked God to forgive me. But the truth was riveting itself upon my mind.

"I came to where I found that a plot was being formed against him. I went on still further to where I witnessed his trial. When I reached the greatest tragedy of all, the crucifixion of Jesus, and heard the scoffing, and saw him nailed to the cross, saw the forehead of the one I had begun to love bleeding from the thorns that pricked it, I said, 'They will never kill him, they cannot kill him. He will come down and defeat them yet!'

"I read on almost breathlessly with fear and yet with hope, and when he bowed his head and died, I closed the book and returned it to the young woman.

" 'I told you that I was full of sorrow. You brought me this book and said that by means of it you would introduce me to someone who would comfort me. You are welcome to your book. Your Christ is a dead Christ, but when our Messiah comes, he will be a living Messiah.'

"The young woman said, 'There's more to the story. Won't you read further?'

"I read of the first Easter morning, the resurrection of Christ; of his victory over the grave; of his speaking to Mary; and of his appearing to his disciples. Then I sank to my knees beside my bed, with the New Testament open, and raising my hands to heaven said, 'O God, I believe that Jesus is the Messiah!'

"I went home, restored to health.

"Mother said, 'You are looking well. Are you engaged?'

"Something better than that, Mother. You will not misunderstand me, will you? I have found the Messiah!'

"Mother said, 'Do you mean to say that you are going to bring upon me a greater sorrow and disgrace than any other?'

"I replied, 'Mother, will you read this book?'

"She took it from my hand, but in a few hours she said, 'Here is your book. You must never ask me to read it again, for it frightens me. I was born into a proud Jewish home, and I must die as I was born. If you ever speak of this again, you will have to leave.' "

Caroline Jonas was silent for six months. Then the time came for the celebration of the Cup Day of Melbourne, when people come from America and all parts of the world and the city runs wild.

The mother said, "Caroline, come with us this afternoon."

"No," she replied, "I cannot."

Rising from the table, her mother said, "You have never been what you used to be since you read that book about your Christ."

Caroline replied, "The time has come when I must confess that he is the Messiah."

She had said all that was necessary. Caroline left her home and stood alone on the sidewalk. She hailed a cab. Looking back to her home—hers no longer—she saw the windows were closed, the blinds drawn, the doors shut. There were her mother, her brother and sister, and fortune.

Then came the thought, "Suppose, after all, that he is not the Messiah!"

But instantly there was a new love in her heart, and a new light in her soul, and she answered the doubt with, "There is no supposing! He is the Messiah!"

The cabman approached her and said:

"Where shall I drive you?"

She stood for a moment and looked about her, and then shrank back in awful dismay, saying, "I don't know."

"But," said the man, "I must take you somewhere."

Suddenly there came to her, she knew not how, a name —The Reverend Dr. Robinson. She did not know where he lived, but she said:

"Drive me to Reverend Dr. Robinson's home."

"Certainly," said the cabman, and soon he stopped near a door bearing a brass plate, on which she read, "Rev. John Robinson, D.D."

She was admitted, and there came to meet her an elderly gentleman in clerical garb.

She asked, "Are you Dr. Robinson?"

"Yes."

"I am a Jewess. My name is Caroline Jonas. I have accepted Jesus as my Messiah. I am alone and without money. I believe God has sent me to you. Will you help me?"

"Will I help you? Why, bless your dear heart, we are just needing a daughter in our home."

He then called out, "My dear, come down."

In a few moments his wife entered the room. He repeated the story of Caroline, adding;

"She wants to know if we will help her."

"Will we help you?" she said, putting her arm around her. "You have left one mother, but you have found another."

Then Caroline Jonas said in her heart:

"There is no supposing. He is the Messiah! Oh! he is the Messiah!"

*   *   *

Caroline Jonas crossed my path when I was looking for a competent woman to take the superintendency of the Home for Women, a department of the great Central Methodist Mission of Melbourne.

I had heard of the fine work done by Miss Jonas in the Melbourne Hospital and of her devotion to her Lord, and almost immediately the thought came to me, "This is the woman for whom I am looking."

"It is you I want," I said, "and you have to come."

"What for?" she asked in surprise.

"To take charge of forty of the worst women that were ever inside or outside of jail; poor, wretched, outcast sisters of the night. Will you come?"

"I don't know how to do such work."

"Never mind, I know something about it. I've been working with them for years. I will teach you. Will you come?"

"Yes."

I afterwards saw that delicate, refined, young Jewess as she paced up and down the room at night with a frenzied opium eater, a drunken, outcast creature, who was raving and tearing her hair.

Caroline said to me, "Lock me in with this woman all night."

I said, "I'm afraid to. I have to leave."

"Lock the door, or we shall not save her, and save her we must."

All night long this woman screamed and tore her hair. I am stating what is true when I say that she literally pulled it out by the roots. She cursed the Jewess and said:

"I will kill you if you don't let me out. But you won't let me out, will you?"

"No, I will not."

And all night Caroline Jonas paced up and down with the frenzied woman, repeating, "God loves you. Jesus is the Messiah. He is able to save you. He saved me. Won't you let him save you?"

As the morning broke, the poor, exhausted woman knelt at the bedside with the Jewess beside her, and said:

"Since you love me as you do, I believe in Jesus the Messiah. I know he is able to save me."

And deliverance came to this victim of sin.

As those two went out of that room, there went with them another, and the form of the third was like that of the Son of God. He was Jesus, the Messiah of Caroline Jonas.

Bernard Jean Bettelheim, M.D.

By MARIE GERLACH EINSPRUCH

After receiving his medical degree from the University of Padua, Dr. Bernard Jean Bettelheim, born in Pressburg, Hungary, in 1811, aided in combatting a cholera epidemic which swept through Italy. His interest in research took him to a number of cities in Italy and Greece, and at the invitation of Mohammed Ali, went to Egypt where he became a naval physician.

Bettelheim was born into an Orthodox Jewish family, and received the traditional Jewish eduction. Always interested in religion, he was involved in a number of discussions and debates with learned rabbis, and even wrote a pamphlet in French about the Talmud. His studies eventually led him to accept Christianity.

As a physician, Dr. Bettelheim went to Japan, although at that time the country still forbade the entrance of foreigners, and having accepted Jesus as his Messiah, he also preached and taught his faith.

From 1845 to 1854 he and his wife worked among the people, in spite of untold hardships. About this time Commodore Matthew Calbraith Perry opened up Japan to the Western world, and Dr. Bettelheim greatly aided him by translating documents into Japanese.

DEDICATION OF MONUMENT AT RYUKU, JAPAN

ON MAY 18, 1926

TO COMMEMORATE THE WORK OF
BERNARD JEAN BETTELHEIM, M.D.

The stand in center supports a gift from the Imperial Household. Mr. Kamii, Governor of the Province; Mr. Kishimoto, Mayor of Naha; Dr. Inouye, President of the Provincial Association of Doctors; officials and people of all classes gathered to honor the memory of a Christian Jew.

A talented linguist, Bettelheim was proficient in twenty-eight languages. He made the first translation of parts of the Bible into Chinese and Japanese, and also compiled a Japanese grammar and dictionary.

Bishop Juji Nakada of Tokyo said: "As far as I am able to learn, Dr. Bettelheim was the first Protestant missionary to Japan. He was a Hungarian Jew who found the Lord at Smyrna. He spent ten years on our islands, during which time he translated the greater part of the New Testament."

He was given passage to the United States by Commodore Perry, and during the Civil War served as surgeon and army physician.

The influence of Dr. Bettelheim in Japan, at the very beginning of Christian missionary work, has not been forgotten, and in 1926, fifty-seven years after his death, a monument was erected to him in recognition of his contribution as physician, translator, and teacher.

Isaiah 53

Who has believed what we have heard? And to whom has the arm of the Lord been revealed?

For he grew up before him like a tender plant, and like a root out of dry ground; he had no form nor comeliness that we should look at him, and no beauty that we should desire him.

He was despised and rejected by men; a man of sorrows and acquainted with grief; and as one from whom men hid their faces, he was despised and we esteemed him not.

Surely he has borne our griefs and carried our sorrows; yet we esteemed him stricken, smitten by God and afflicted.

But he was wounded for our transgressions, he was bruised for our iniquities; the chastisement of our peace was upon him, and with his stripes we are healed.

All we like sheep have gone astray; we have turned every one to his own way; and the Lord has laid on him the iniquity of us all.

He was oppressed and he was afflicted, yet he opened not his mouth; like a lamb that is led to the slaughter, and like a sheep that before its shearers is dumb, so he opened not his mouth.

By oppression and judgment he was taken away; and as for his generation, who considered that he was cut off out of the land of the living, stricken for the transgression of my people?

And they made his grave with the wicked, and with the rich his tomb; although he had done no violence, and there was no deceit in his mouth.

Yet it pleased the Lord to bruise him; he has put him to grief; when you shall make his soul an offering for sin, he shall see his seed, he shall prolong his days, and the pleasure of the Lord shall prosper in his hand.

He shall see of the travail of his soul and be satisfied; by his knowledge shall the righteous one, my servant, justify many, and he shall bear their iniquities.

Therefore will I divide him a portion with the great, and he shall divide the spoil with the strong; because he poured out his soul unto death, and was numbered with the transgressors; yet he bore the sin of many, and made intercession with the transgressors.

ישעיה נ"ג

מִי הֶאֱמִין לִשְׁמֻעָתֵנוּ וּזְרוֹעַ יְהוָה עַל־מִי נִגְלָתָה: וַיַּעַל
כַּיּוֹנֵק לְפָנָיו וְכַשֹּׁרֶשׁ מֵאֶרֶץ צִיָּה לֹא־תֹאַר לוֹ וְלֹא הָדָר
וְנִרְאֵהוּ וְלֹא־מַרְאֶה וְנֶחְמְדֵהוּ: נִבְזֶה וַחֲדַל אִישִׁים אִישׁ
מַכְאֹבוֹת וִידוּעַ חֹלִי וּכְמַסְתֵּר פָּנִים מִמֶּנּוּ נִבְזֶה וְלֹא חֲשַׁבְנֻהוּ:
אָכֵן חֳלָיֵנוּ הוּא נָשָׂא וּמַכְאֹבֵינוּ סְבָלָם וַאֲנַחְנוּ חֲשַׁבְנֻהוּ נָגוּעַ
מֻכֵּה אֱלֹהִים וּמְעֻנֶּה: וְהוּא מְחֹלָל מִפְּשָׁעֵנוּ מְדֻכָּא מֵעֲוֺנֹתֵינוּ
מוּסַר שְׁלוֹמֵנוּ עָלָיו וּבַחֲבֻרָתוֹ נִרְפָּא־לָנוּ: כֻּלָּנוּ כַּצֹּאן תָּעִינוּ
אִישׁ לְדַרְכּוֹ פָּנִינוּ וַיהוָה הִפְגִּיעַ בּוֹ אֵת עֲוֺן כֻּלָּנוּ: נִגַּשׂ וְהוּא
נַעֲנֶה וְלֹא יִפְתַּח־פִּיו כַּשֶּׂה לַטֶּבַח יוּבָל וּכְרָחֵל לִפְנֵי גֹזְזֶיהָ
נֶאֱלָמָה וְלֹא יִפְתַּח פִּיו: מֵעֹצֶר וּמִמִּשְׁפָּט לֻקָּח וְאֶת־דּוֹרוֹ
מִי יְשׂוֹחֵחַ כִּי נִגְזַר מֵאֶרֶץ חַיִּים מִפֶּשַׁע עַמִּי נֶגַע לָמוֹ: וַיִּתֵּן
אֶת־רְשָׁעִים קִבְרוֹ וְאֶת־עָשִׁיר בְּמֹתָיו עַל לֹא־חָמָס עָשָׂה
וְלֹא מִרְמָה בְּפִיו: וַיהוָה חָפֵץ דַּכְּאוֹ הֶחֱלִי אִם־תָּשִׂים אָשָׁם
נַפְשׁוֹ יִרְאֶה זֶרַע יַאֲרִיךְ יָמִים וְחֵפֶץ יְהוָה בְּיָדוֹ יִצְלָח: מֵעֲמַל
נַפְשׁוֹ יִרְאֶה יִשְׂבָּע בְּדַעְתּוֹ יַצְדִּיק צַדִּיק עַבְדִּי לָרַבִּים וַעֲוֺנֹתָם
הוּא יִסְבֹּל: לָכֵן אֲחַלֶּק־לוֹ בָרַבִּים וְאֶת־עֲצוּמִים יְחַלֵּק
שָׁלָל תַּחַת אֲשֶׁר הֶעֱרָה לַמָּוֶת נַפְשׁוֹ וְאֶת־פֹּשְׁעִים נִמְנָה וְהוּא
חֵטְא־רַבִּים נָשָׂא וְלַפֹּשְׁעִים יַפְגִּיעַ:

און ער האָט געמאַכט זיַן קֶבר מיט רשָעים און ריַיכע, הַגם
ער האָט קיין אומרעכט נישט געטאָן, און קיין פֿאַלשקיַיט איז נישט
געווען אין זיַן מויל.

אָבער גאָט האָט אים געוואָלט צעשטויסן דורך קראַנקשאַפֿט.
ווען ער וועט מאַכן זיַן נֶפֶש אַ קָרבן, וועט ער זען זאַמען און פֿאַר־
לענגערן זיַינע טעג, און דער רָצון פֿון גאָט וועט אין זיַן האַנט
באַגליקן.

ליַידן פֿון זיַן נֶפֶש וועט ער זיך אָנזען צו זאַט; מיט זיַן דער־
קֶענונג וועט מיַן גערעכטער קנעכט גערעכט מאַכן אַ סַך, און זייערע
זינד וועט ער טראָגן.

דעריבער וועל איך אים געבן אַ חֶלֶק צווישן די גרויסע, און
מיט די מעכטיקע וועט ער טיילן רויב; דערפֿאַר וואָס ער האָט
אויסגעגאָסן זיַן נשמה צום טויט, און איז געציילט געוואָרן מיט פֿאַר־
ברעכער, בעת ער האָט געטראָגן דעם חֵטא פֿון אַ סַך, און זיך
אָנגענומען פֿאַר די פֿאַרברעכער.

ישעיה נ"ג

ווער האָט געגלויבט וואָס מיר האָבן געהערט, און צו וועמען
איז דער אָרעם פון גאָט אַנטפּלעקט געוואָרן?

וואָרים ער איז אויפגעגאַנגען ווי אַ יונג צוויַיגל פאַר אים, און
ווי אַ וואָרצל פון טרוקענער ערד; ער האָט נישט געהאַט קיין געשטאַלט
און קיין שיינקייט, אַז מיר זאָלן קוקן אויף אים, און קיין אויסזען, אַז
ער זאָל אונדז געפעלן.

ער איז געווען פאַראַכט און אויסגעמיטן פון מענטשן, אַ מענטש
פון פּיַין און געוואוינט צו קראַנקהייט, און ווי אַיינער פון וועמען
מענטשן קערן אָפּ זייער פּנים; ער איז געווען פאַראַכט און מיר האָבן
אים נישט געשוינט.

פאַרוואָר, ער האָט געליטן אונדזערע קראַנקהייטן, און אונדזערע
וויטאַקן האָט ער געטראָגן; מיר אָבער האָבן אים געהאַלטן פאַר אַ
געפּלאָגטן פון גאָט, געשלאָגן און געפּיַיניקט.

אָבער ער איז געווען פאַרוואונדעט צוליב אונדזער זינד, און
צעשטויסן צוליב אונדזער אומגערעכטיקייט; די שטראָף פון אונדזער
שלום איז געווען אויף אים, און דורך זיַינע ביַילן זענען מיר געהיילט
געוואָרן.

מיר אַלע האָבן ווי שאָף פאַרבלאָנדזשעט, איטלעכער האָט זיך
געקערט צו זיַין אייגענעם וועג; און גאָט האָט געלאָזט טרעפן אויף
אים די זינד פון אונדז אַלעמען.

ער איז געוואָרן געפּיַיניקט, און בעת ער האָט זיך געבויגן האָט
ער זיַין מויל נישט געעפנט; ווי אַ לאַם וואָס ווערט געפירט צו דער
שחיטה, און ווי אַ שאָף איז שטום פאַר איר שערער, האָט ער זיַין
מויל נישט געעפנט.

דורך דריקונג און שטראָף איז ער אַוועקגענומען געוואָרן, און
ווער פון זיַין דור טוט גאָר קלערן, אַז ער איז פאַרשניטן געוואָרן פון
לאַנד פון די לעבעדיקע, פאַר די זינד פון מיַין פאָלק, וואָס האָט
די שטראָף פאַרדינט.

A Jewish Crusader

In Brazil

By JOHN STUART CONNING

"To whom does the prophet refer in this chapter?"

The question was asked by a Jewish boy of fourteen of his rabbi father. *Sukkoth*, the Feast of Tabernacles, was being celebrated, and in the booth which had been erected for its observance sat a company of the Rabbi's followers. On the table lay a number of books, among them a well-used copy of the Prophets. It was this book which the boy, now considered old enough to listen to the discussions of his elders, casually took up and which opened easily at a passage that had evidently been often examined—the fifty-third chapter of Isaiah. On the margin were numerous notes. Among them a question loomed out: "To whom does the prophet refer in this chapter?"

Innocently, the boy turned to his father and repeated the question. The father looked at his son as if startled, and a stillness fell upon the company. Not receiving an answer, the boy again repeated the question, and to his amazement and confusion his father snatched the book from his hand.

In such an atmosphere of unquestioning and uncompromising orthodoxy, Solomon L. Ginsburg was born in the city of Suwalki, Poland. Previous to this experience he had been sent at six years of age to the home of his mother in Koenigsberg, Germany, that he might secure a higher education than was possible for a Jewish boy in Poland. His mother's father was a well-to-do merchant, learned, widely travelled, who frequently took the boy with him on his journeys. When he reached the age of fourteen, his father insisted upon his return to Suwalki.

Coming back to the rigid forms of traditional Judaism, there was aroused in young Ginsburg an attitude of incipient revolt. This was further stimulated by the determination of his father to make him a Jewish teacher. In order to further this plan, he was to marry the daughter of a wealthy Jewish family who would support him for seven years until his education was complete. He was vexed at the total disregard of his own wishes in the matter and with the open commercialism of it all, and determined to escape. When the bride chosen for him was twelve years of age and he fifteen, and the preparations were under way for the wedding, he ran away.

After many wanderings and varied experiences, he found his way to London where an uncle, his mother's brother, gladly received him and gave him a position in his large dry goods store. It was while in London that an incident took place which changed his whole life.

Passing through the Whitechapel district on a Saturday afternoon, he met a man who invited him to go to the Mildmay Mission to hear an explanation of the fifty-third chapter of Isaiah. At once there flashed before him the scene in the booth during *Sukkoth* in Poland. Prompted by curiosity he decided to go.

There was much in the explanation of the chapter that he did not understand, yet it made a profound impression on him. A three-month struggle ensued. During this time he read the New Testament and came to the conviction that Jesus of Nazareth was indeed the Messiah of his people.

He well knew the consequences that would follow an

avowal of his faith in Jesus, and the final step was taken at a meeting at which John Wilkinson of the Mildmay Mission spoke on *Matthew* 10:37: "He that loveth father or mother more than me is not worthy of me."

"Not worthy of me"—he emphasized the words until their insistence searched the soul of the young man. At last, overwhelmed with conviction, he rose and said with trembling voice: "I want to be worthy of Jesus."

The decision made that night brought him peace and joy. Tears of happiness and gratitude were in his eyes when at last refreshing sleep came to him.

With that decisiveness which characterized his whole life, he was not long in confessing his new-found faith. At the breakfast table next morning his uncle, noticing his radiant face, said:

"Solomon, why do you look so happy this morning?"

At once he replied: "Uncle, for the past three months I have been going through a great struggle."

He told of his contact with Christians, of his reading the New Testament, and finished by saying:

"Last night I made my decision and have accepted Jesus as my Messiah."

All efforts to induce him to change his mind were unavailing, and in consequence he left his uncle's home. A year passed in which he had no communication with his people. Then he received a note from another uncle telling him that he had come to London on business and would like to see him. Gladly he accepted the invitation. After the greeting and receiving news of his home, the uncle said:

"Do you know why I came to London?"

"Yes, on business, as you said."

"That is true. I had some business to do, but my real business is to take you back home."

"That is great! I am ready to go with you any time."

"I know that you are ready, but there is one condition

you must meet—you must leave your new religion behind. I will give you a week to make your decision."

"Oh, the horror of that long, seemingly never-ending week!" he declared afterward. "It was a week of terrible trial and temptation, and had it not been for the Lord himself, I would surely have failed."

But time, however slowly it may drag, brings at last the appointed day. Young Ginsburg was called to meet his uncles, and with them were several white-bearded elders of Israel. They reasoned and pled with him to give up his Christian faith, but with no success.

Like many others before him, the entrance into the new faith was like passing from the dark hour before the dawn into the full-tide glory of the morning light. He was eager to tell others the good news and took advantage of every opportunity to proclaim his belief, especially among his own people.

After three years in a training home where he learned the printer's trade, and another three years in a Bible college, a call came to go as a missionary to Brazil, which he accepted. He was sent to Portugal to study the language, staying with the family of a merchant from Brazil who had come to Portugal to recover from the effects of the tropical heat.

The facility of young Ginsburg in learning the Portuguese language, and his zeal, resourcefulness, and courage, may be gathered from the fact that at the end of the first month in Portugal, he wrote a tract in English, translated it into Portuguese, had it printed, and went about the country selling it. He sold three thousand copies.

The story of Solomon Ginsburg's work as a missionary in Brazil reads like a modern edition of the Acts of the Apostles. The following incident may be cited to illustrate the spirit of this dauntless man:

In the northern part of the State of Pernambuco there was a band of brigands roving about who were guilty of all sorts of atrocities. The chief of the band was one of the most daring men that ever appeared in Brazil. The government had offered 40,000 milreis for his apprehension, but so deadly was his aim that none dared to attack him. This man, Antonio Silvino by name, had been hired for fifty dollars to kill Ginsburg, whose character and work were deliberately misrepresented to him. Some of Ginsburg's friends learned of the plot to assassinate him, and sought to warn him of the danger, but were unable to reach him.

One morning, on his way to the village of Moganga, he saw a slender, wiry-looking man standing in a field by the road with a double-barrelled gun in his hand and a long chain of cartridges across his chest. As was his custom, Ginsburg stopped to greet the stranger, wishing him good morning and inquiring pleasantly as to his success in hunting. The man seemed reluctant to reply, so with a cheerful word of farewell, Ginsburg put spurs to his horse and started off. As he did so, a man sprang from behind a tree and tried to grasp the bridle of his horse, but in response to a shout from the man with the gun, he jumped aside and let Ginsburg continue his journey.

A few hours later, when he reached the village where he was scheduled to speak, he was bewildered by the looks of surprise on the faces of those who greeted him. The friend with whom he was to stay asked him eagerly:

"Did you meet Antonio Silvino?"

On asking for a decription of the man, he realized that the notorious brigand was none other than the man he had greeted by the wayside.

Rejoicing in his deliverance, and wondering why he had escaped the assassin's bullet, he went about the duties that filled the day. Finally, wearied from his labors, he went to the home where he was to stay, and soon after he entered, there came a loud knocking at the door and a demand that it be opened. When the host set the door ajar, great was his trepidation to find himself confronted by the desperado, Antonio Silvino, who demanded to see his guest. Casting himself upon the Lord for protection, Ginsburg went to meet him. His host was trembling, and his wife and sister were weeping and wringing their hands.

Walking up to the intruder, the missionary said quietly:
"You wished to see me, what can I do for you?"

"Do you know who I am?" the bandit asked, after a little hesitation.

"Yes," replied Ginsburg, "you are Captain Antonio Silvino."

"Do you know why I came here?"

"Yes, you have been hired to kill me."

"That is true," he replied.

For several minutes Ginsburg stood waiting for some word or act from the outlaw. Then addressing him again, he asked:

"Then why don't you go ahead and do it?"

Silvino looked up and said: "No, I won't kill a man like you. This morning, as I was waiting for you near the Sape village, you stopped your horse and spoke to me so gentlemanly and kindly that I was surprised. I was told that you were a dangerous person, that your teachings were a curse to the people and to the country, and that killing you would be a good thing. But when you spoke to me in so friendly a way, I determined to find out more about you. I was present today when you were preaching and teaching and singing and praying, and I tell you I am not going to kill one who is doing such good work. I would much rather kill the man who hired me to kill you."

They spent the night together, bandit and preacher, talking and praying. Antonio told him the story of his life. He belonged to a wealthy, aristocratic family. On account of political feuds, most of his people had been slain. Incensed against society, he entered a career of lawlessness. But that night with Ginsburg marked the beginning of a new era in his life. He was completely transformed. He gave up his old ways, became an ardent witness for Christ, and a friend and protector of the missionary.

Solomon Ginsburg was a true missionary statesman. Early in his work, his zeal to evangelize the people led him to pass quickly from city to city, preaching the Gospel and winning converts. He soon found that these young converts, left without instruction or organization and subjected to bitter persecution, became quiescent followers of Christ. He determined to follow the example of the apostle Paul, staying in a place until he had gathered a company of believers, instructing them in the faith, organizing a church, and providing them with a preacher. Through this method he was able to establish scores of churches in various parts of Brazil which became centers of evangelism.

In many cities and towns of Brazil the name of Solomon Ginsburg is held in deepest reverence as a true apostle of Jesus Christ. In some communities as many as a thousand persons in a single year were won to the discipleship of Christ.

Ginsburg's printing experience in London led him to place a high value on the printed page. At the beginning of his ministry in Campos he purchased a small press and a few fonts of type, and began the publication of a little monthly which he called Boas Novas ("Good News"). This work grew steadily in volume and usefulness. Later, the publishing business of the various mission stations was unified and taken to Rio de Janeiro, and he was asked to give special attention to this work. The Carroll Memorial Press, with the stream of literature that flows from it into all parts of Brazil, is an abiding monument to the vision, faith, and ability of Solomon Ginsburg.

He knew how to make friends. "Pastor Solomon" was the title affectionately given to him by his associates. From among his converts many were trained for leadership among their own people, and such men as Joaquim Fernandes Lessa, Andrian Onesimo Bernardo, and Manoel Avelino de Souza, who are mighty for God in their native country, bear eloquent testimony to the inspiring leadership of Pastor Solomon.

In the midst of constant difficulty and danger, Ginsburg learned to live trustfully. His thrilling experiences with mobs who had been incited to fury against his preaching of the Gospel, and his marvelous escapes from the knife and bullet of the assassin, made him realize continually that the care of God for his servants was not confined to apostolic times, when angel hands opened prison doors and unseen guards preserved from surrounding perils.

One day, when Ginsburg was preaching in a hall in Pernambuco, there came in a great giant of a man named Herculano. The message was about Christ's power to deliver from the guilt and thralldom of sin. Herculano listened with amazement. Never before had he heard such words. At the close of the service he lingered, and the missionary, recognizing that he had been impressed, asked him if he would like to have him visit his home in order to go into these matters more carefully. He readily assented, and a meeting was arranged for the next day.

On being told where he was going, Ginsburg's friends tried to dissuade him from making the visit. He was informed that Herculano was a desperate character, guilty of the most atrocious crimes, that his place was one of the most dangerous in Pernambuco—a veritable den of thieves and murderers that even the police would not dream of going to alone, and that strangers who ventured there were seldom heard from again.

But, having given his word to the man, Ginsburg resolved to keep his promise and trust in God for protection.

At the appointed time and place he met the great Hercules of a Brazilian, who led him over a small rickety foot-bridge into the dangerous district. People who saw him going with Herculano turned and looked after him with surprise at his temerity, some with pity, never expecting that he would return.

When they reached the adobe hut, the home of Herculano, every living thing seemed to disappear—his wife and children, the dogs and cats—all seemed to fear his presence and flee for their lives.

As Ginsburg seated himself upon an old kerosene can, he could not help noticing the bloodshot, murderous features of the man into whose home he had entered. Realizing his position, and that this was perhaps the last opportunity to speak of Christ's redeeming power, he resolved to speak plainly.

"My dear friend," he said, "I really do not know who you are or what you intend doing with me. I was warned of the kind of people who live here, of the danger of coming to this place, and of what has happened to many a stranger who has been lured here. But as I noticed last night your hunger for something better, and your desire to learn more about Jesus and his power to save, I resolved to come and tell you about these things even at the risk of my life. Personally I am not afraid to die; I am more concerned about your soul than I am about my own life."

As he talked, the man turned pale and his big body trembled as if in the grip of some compelling emotion. He confessed afterwards that he was struggling with himself not to fall on his visitor and strangle him, as he had done with others many times before, but that something, some invisible power, held him back and would not let him move.

At length his agitation passed and he said quietly:

"What you spoke about last night disturbed my sleep. I wondered if what you said was really true. I have never heard anything like it."

In simple words Ginsburg told the old story of God's love in Christ, of how his redeeming power is given to those who repent and forsake sin and turn to him for pardon. But the words seemed to fall on barren soil. As he looked at the poor fellow sitting in bewilderment, his eyes mirroring the torment of a despairing soul, he turned to him and said:

"My dear friend, I see that you do not understand my words. Let us ask God to make these things plain to you.

If you really want to know the truth of what I have been saying, kneel down with me and ask God to show you the truth and save you."

As he slipped to his knees, the big giant, who very likely had never before in his life bent his knees before his Maker, knelt beside him. Then, with trembling voice and eyes overflowing with tears, the man of God began pleading in prayer for the poor benighted soul.

The answer came speedily. The giant fell prostrate to the floor, and with choked voice, in an agony of sorrow and despair, wailed piteously over and over: "O God, have mercy on a poor, degraded, miserable sinner!"

Peace came at last as Ginsburg repeated the great assurances of God's infinite compassion and of his mercy to the uttermost. Then with tears of penitence, of shame and sorrow, Herculano, by the power of God, entered upon a new life. He became a powerful instrument for his Master, and his home became a center of spiritual influence which permeated the whole district.

Out of such experiences Solomon L. Ginsburg learned the lesson of implicit trust in God. He was able to say: "Be the future what it may, God will direct it aright and keep me from all harm in the path wherein he wants me to walk."

In the midst of his labors, still dreaming of further conquests for Christ, he received the call to higher service. He died on the first of April, 1927, after thirty-three years of sacrificial effort for Brazil, leaving behind a notable record of achievement.

The Southern Baptist Convention of the United States, under whose auspices he labored, speaks of him as "decidedly the greatest all-around missionary in Brazil."

Ginsburg needs no monument. His memorials are scattered over the hills and valleys and plains of Brazil, in Churches that, in the midst of ignorance and superstition, witness to a living faith, and in a multitude of lives brought under the sway of Christ through his testimony.

A Tiberias Rabbi

By W. M. CHRISTIE

From the second century C.E., Tiberias by the Sea of Galilee was the seat of the Jewish Patriarchate, and at that time the greatest center of Jewish learning. It gave the world the Mishnah in 188 C.E., the Jerusalem Talmud in 360 C.E., the Revised Hebrew Bible in 552 C.E., and that magnificent work, the Massoretic pointing, in 150 C.E. It has maintained its position and place of dignity down to our own day, and few titles could command respect like that of "A Tiberias Rabbi."

In such an atmosphere Ephraim ben Joseph Eliakim was born. His father was a rabbi in the old city, a leading man in the Arabic-speaking Jewish community. Following the rabbinical maxim that a boy should take up the occupation of his father (*Arachin*, 16b), Ephraim was from the first destined for the rabbi's chair, and became a diligent student in Bible and Talmudic subjects. In due time he attained the dignity of *Haham*, the usual designation for rabbi.

Esteemed and honored by Jews and Arabs alike, he held a leading place in the community, and became one of the *dayanim*, overseers of justice, who are specially entrusted with the rights and interests of the individuals of the community.

Coincident with these advances, he married the daughter of the Chief Rabbi, and as the family had in some way acquired French protection, he had good reason to look forward to a life of comfort and freedom.

Haham Ephraim

Along with other duties, Rabbi Ephraim undertook the teaching of the Bible and the Talmud. His school was of the kind usual in Tiberias in the last decade of the last century. The rabbi had his chair and the pupils sat around on mats on the floor, literally at the feet of their master. Generally the Bible was studied only through the Talmud, but the Bible for its own sake attracted him, and received more than ordinary attention from him.

Haham Ephraim was wary of Christians, especially missionaries, and would not venture near them. In his own words he said that he had "never permitted his wife or children to go near the hospital department of the Church of Scotland Mission, however ill they might be," a compromise most of the other rabbis were ready to make whenever a Jewish doctor was not available.

But a change was to come. The head of the Church of Scotland in Tiberias at that time was the Rev. Dr. William Ewing. During a visit to the Jewish section of the town, I accompanied him. On our way the school of Haham Ephraim was passed, and we looked in through the open window. Dr. Ewing, facile in Hebrew, greeted the Rabbi. Kindly words from one he had been accustomed to look upon with fear and distrust, touched the Rabbi's heart, and a few days later he appeared at Dr. Ewing's home.

The two men were of almost equal age, and very soon the formal visit developed into friendly talk. Many different subjects were discussed, with the Talmud and the Bible having a prominent place. The Haham called upon Dr. Ewing again and again, and every conversation led from both sides to the claims of Jesus as Messiah. The Rabbi's knowledge of the Bible stood him in good stead, and the prophecies gradually became clearer to him.

The older Jewish interpretation of the fifty-third chapter of Isaiah was known as referring to the King Messiah. It was not long before Haham Ephraim recognized the picture of the Suffering Servant "by whose stripes we are healed." The sufferings of his own people throughout the ages touched him deeply. He looked back through the centuries and asked: "Where are the promises to the fathers? We are God's chosen people, the glorious things that were to be ours are the possession of strangers."

Guided by Dr. Ewing, the Haham considered: "The first temple was destroyed and the nation scattered on account of three great sins committed by Israel, but seventy years later the temple was rebuilt. Then came the second destruction, and for over eighteen hundred years Israel has been without the Holy House. What was the cause of this second destruction and of the greater scattering? Idolatry was not the reason. There was no lack of zeal for either the Law or the sacrifices. Men were zealous for God and did not cease the temple service till the hour of destruction came. Why has God forsaken us so long?"

The Haham wept and prayed and struggled with the problem, unwilling to give in. He even asked questions about these things of his brother rabbis, but they could give only the time-worn formal answers of traditional Judaism. He was still unsatisfied, and the only result of his queries was to arouse suspicion among his brother rabbis who set a closer watch upon his movements.

Still he struggled, convinced that some terrible sin had been the cause of the wrath of God against his people. Then there dawned on him the secret of it all—"hatred without a cause" (Yoma 9b). A still, small voice expostulated within him, "Cease to hate Me. Love Me and I will give you peace."

The struggle was over. Rabbi Ephraim found a peace that was unbroken till his dying day.

At the thought of the next scene I still shudder. Rabbi Ephraim told his family that he was going to Jaffa for a few days. He was suspected and set upon, but found refuge with Dr. Ewing. It was decided that Dr. Ewing, the Rabbi and I start for Jaffa before dawn the next morning. We had just got clear of the old castle when we were surrounded by a raving crowd, immediately unhorsed, and Ephraim was almost torn to pieces. Dr. Ewing talked to the crowd, and they finally dispersed.

A conference was then held in which the Haham's wife and one or two rabbis took part, but it was suddenly broken up, and the Haham let it be known that the journey to Jaffa was off. He took his wife's arm and walked home with her.

Then began a time of fierce persecution. Rabbi Ephraim was secretly and suddenly seized. Afterwards it became known that a false accusation of theft had been brought against him, and that he had been confined in a filthy cell. His resolution and spirit remained unbroken. He was flogged and starved, a punishment which injured his health for life. Still he was true to his convictions.

Condemned as a traitor, he was secretly removed from the town to a Jewish colony at the Waters of Meron (Lake Huleh), and his name blotted out of the remembrance of his friends and companions.

Months later one of the workers of the hospital at Tiberias, while riding in the Upper Jordan Valley, saw a forlorn figure bending to his task in the field under a hot sun. On closer approach he was surprised to find it was none other than Rabbi Ephraim. He was greatly changed. The hardships he had endured had left their marks upon his frame. The lines had deepened on his weather-beaten features, but there was a light of eager welcome in his eyes.

In answer to questions, he told briefly of his experiences. But these things had not moved him. Nothing daunted, he held on his way. A return to Tiberias was then impossible, and for support he willingly endured the weariness of unwonted toil until it should please God to make his duty plain. He stood among the furrows in the field, waving a genial farewell to his departing friend. Then, heartened by the interview, he bent afresh to his labor.

Not long afterwards Rabbi Ephraim turned up in

Nazareth, and there was baptized. He soon learned what great things he must suffer for Christ's sake. Upon his return to Tiberias his wife and children were taken from him. Though his wife loved him dearly, the relatives on both sides of the house united in threats and warnings, and kept the closest observation on her movements.

"Had he been an ordinary Jew," they said in my hearing, "we could have understood it. But that a rabbi, and one of his standing, should change, why, we never heard of such a thing."

His children were young, and were kept beyond his influence. However, they were continually on his heart, and were constantly in his intercessions. In matters of faith, however, the rabbinical barrier was maintained, and there was little association, except with the oldest son during a period of World War I.

The Haham made his way to Jerusalem. Suspicion and misrepresentation dogged his path, and he was misunderstood by nearly everybody. He worked as a day laborer, carrying stones and mortar. His income was that of an ordinary worker, but he never complained. He was content with the simplest of living and clothing, and anything he could spare from his meager resources he used to help the poor whom he met through his continual testimony to the Gospel. Thus his service was not only in word, but also in deed.

During this time he came much in contact with the rabbis in Jerusalem, many of whom had been his pupils in Tiberias. They were troubled and vexed to find him doing such lowly work, and pled with him: "We beg you to have regard for your age and to abandon this hard and menial labor and return with us to be our father and chief as you were formerly."

He accepted their offers of friendship with thankfulness, for they were evidences of their love for their old teacher. But he remained unswerving in his loyalty to his Messiah.

A happy change came when he was appointed as an evangelist in the service of the Christian and Missionary

Alliance, nearer to the center of Jerusalem and to those he was anxious to reach. Freed from hard manual labor, he could now devote his whole time and strength to witnessing among his fellow Jews. The Alliance rented a meeting-room for him on the Jaffa Road, and there many a warm disputation took place. This sometimes led to his being stoned, and on one occasion he received an ugly gash on the head. But still he never thought of ceasing to praise his Messiah, and the meeting-room was often filled to overflowing for the Saturday evening service.

Efforts were again made to secure his recantation, or at least his silence. Persecution had failed. Flattery and tempting inducements were resorted to. He was invited out by the rabbis, and he accepted the invitations, even to the Chief Rabbinate, for thereby he got what his heart yearned for most—the opportunity of proclaiming the Gospel.

Haham Ephraim spent hours with the rabbis, reasoning with them from the Scriptures that Jesus is the Messiah. The majority remained unconvinced, but some of them were awakened, recognized the proofs he presented, and met him privately from time to time for study and prayer.

I met him again in the summer of 1927, a joyful and happy reunion after thirty-four years. He was steadfast in the faith, humble and contented. His association with the Alliance was now continued in a voluntary way. It gave him great joy to spend a portion of his Sabbath day in the Reading Room, which bore the designation *Beth Dorshe Emeth*, the House of the Seekers After Truth. As men and boys came in, he talked with them, and very often remained for the evening meeting, carrying through the Service in Hebrew, which by this time was again a living language in the land. In all things he was an outstanding testimony to the saving power of the Messiah Jesus.

The Rev. Esber Domet, a close friend of Haham Ephraim, gives a beautiful account of their last talk together the evening before he was called Home. He wrote: "I felt the presence of the Lord near that bed. Haham Ephraim asked me to pray with him. After I had done so, he too prayed as follows: 'O Lord Jesus, I praise Thee that Thou hast redeemed me. I bless Thee that Thou didst use me in Thy service for the salvation of many souls. I beseech Thee, Lord Jesus, to bless Thy Church all over the world and to strengthen it. But I especially thank Thee for the many believers here in Jerusalem. Give them faith and courage that they may never falter in their witness. Amen.' ''

With such words and thoughts of praise for the Lord he loved and whom he served so long, he passed from this world to hear the welcome, "Well done, good and faithful servant . . . I will give you a crown of life."

That was on the 30th of August, 1930. The next day the venerable Rabbi, at the age of seventy-four, was laid in his last earthly resting place. Mr. Gabriel, of the Arabic Christian community, records the event: "Another grave was dug alongside of the Haham's for another brother in Christ, of the Arabic race. Jew and Arab were laid one beside the other, and Jews and Arabs, standing with bowed heads by the two open graves, were touched and softened the one toward the other."

Bishop of Jerusalem

By ABRAHAM ZOLONTZ

Michael Solomon Alexander was born in 1799 in Schönlanke, a small manufacturing town in the Grand Duchy of Posen, Germany. His parents were strict Jews, and he was brought up with a strong prejudice against Christianity.

At the age of twenty-one he went to England to continue his calling as a teacher of the Talmud, and also to perform the duties of a *shochet*, a ritual slaughterer. While teaching in the city of Colchester, he noticed a poster advertising a meeting of the "London Society for Promoting Christianity Among the Jews." The very title of the Society aroused his curiosity, as up to this time he did not even know of the existence of the New Testament.

He obtained a copy. Its message gripped him and began to fill his mind with all sorts of doubts and questions, which he sought to resist. About this time he completed his education and was appointed Rabbi of Norwich. Later he moved to Plymouth, where he met and married an attractive young woman, Deborah Levi.

One of the curates of the Plymouth Parish, a Rev. B. B. Golding of the Stonehouse Church, came to Rabbi Alexander for Hebrew lessons. In the course of their study, he began to read such passages as Psalm 22 and Isaiah 53. A struggle then began in the soul of the young rabbi. He used to steal down to the Stonehouse Church on Sunday evenings, and under the

Bishop Michael  Solomon Alexander

shadow of its walls would stand riveted to the spot while he listened to the songs of Christian praise.

Rabbi Alexander's congregation soon became aware of his leanings toward Christianity, and he was suspended from his duties as rabbi. Not long after, he made public profession of his faith in the Messiah Jesus, and was baptized at a service attended by over one thousand people.

Unknown to Rabbi Alexander, his wife had also become a secret inquirer, and was baptized six months later.

Michael Alexander was ordained deacon in Dublin in 1827, and later in the same year was ordained priest by the Bishop of Kildare, an occasion which attracted much attention. He joined the staff of the "London Society for Promoting Christianity Among the Jews," and served as missionary in Danzig, as well as in London.

While in London he took an active part in the translation of the Anglican liturgy into Hebrew. He held the post of Professor of Hebrew and Rabbinical Literature in King's College, and also gained distinction in the Jewish community by heading a list of sixty Christian Jews who subscribed to a formal protest against the Blood Accusation, the revival of the wicked and baseless slander accusing Jews of the murder of Christian children in order to use their blood in the Passover ceremonials.

In 1841 Michael Alexander was consecrated Bishop by the Archbishop of Canterbury, the Bishop of London, the Bishop of Rochester, the Bishop of New Zealand, and went out to the Holy Land as the first Protestant Bishop of Jersualem. Here he established daily services, spared not himself from toil and care, and broke down and died in four years time.

The cause of Bishop Alexander's death was doubtless the great and continued anxiety such as the Bishopric of Jerusalem and its cares can best account for. Had he not gone to the East, he might possibly have lived to a good old age, but the mitre of Jerusalem, like the wreath of our blessed Lord, was to him a crown of thorns.

A letter of condolence to Mrs. Alexander, signed by thirty-one Jewish Christians at Jerusalem, was a most eloquent testimony to the blessing which had followed the successful labors of the Bishop. We quote in part:

"Next to yourself and your family, we consider ourselves the chief mourners; for we feel both collectively and individually that we have lost not only a true Father in Christ, but also a loving brother and a most kind friend. The affectionate love he bore to Israel, which peculiarly characterized him, could not fail to render him beloved by everyone who had the privilege of knowing him.

"His exalted piety, and most exemplary life and conversation, inspired the highest reverential esteem. He was a burning and a shining light. When he was raised to the highest dignity in the Church, he conferred the most conspicuous honor on our whole nation, but especially on us Jewish believers. With him, captive Judah's brightest earthly star has set, and the top stone has been taken away from the rising Hebrew Church."

Alexander was the first Jewish Christian to attain to the dignity of the Anglican Episcopate. His friends and those who worked under him loved him for his kind nature—for he had an ear, heart and purse open to all. He was an Israelite indeed in whom there was no guile. His was a strikingly interesting personality, rendered doubly so in that he was a Hebrew of the Hebrews, and in his episcopal dignity, a link with the primitive Hebrew Christian Church in the Mother City of Christendom.

Rabbi Isaac Lichtenstein

By JONATHAN KAMER

He was not yet twenty when he became a rabbi, and after officiating for several years in various communities in northern Hungary, Isaac Lichtenstein finally settled as District Rabbi in Tapio Szele. There he remained for nearly forty years, laboring ceaselessly and unselfishly for the good of his people.

One day a teacher in one of his district schools showed him a German Bible. Turning the pages, Rabbi Lichtenstein's eyes fell on the name "Jesu Christi." He became furiously angry and sharply reproved the teacher for having such a book in his possession. In his rage he flung it across the room, where it fell behind others on a shelf, and lay dusty and forgotten for some thirty-odd years.

During a fierce wave of anti-Semitism in the picturesque little Hungarian town of Tisza Eslar, situated on the Theiss, twelve Jews and a Jewess were thrown into prison, accused of having killed a Christian girl in order to use her blood for ritual purposes. As in every other case in which such a diabolical charge was brought against Jews, the blood accusation in Tisza Eslar was ultimately proven to be false and baseless.

It occurred to Rabbi Lichtenstein that there must be something in the teachings of the New Testament which excited enmity against the Jews, and while browsing among his books he came upon the German Bible which thirty years before he had thrown away in a rage. He picked it up and

Rabbi Isaac Lichtenstein

District Synagogue, Tapio Szele

examined it carefully. The state of his mind at this time is best revealed in his publication, JUDENSPIEGEL, A *Jewish Mirror*, in which he wrote:

" 'Much have they afflicted me from my youth up, let Israel now say' (*Psalm* 129:1). No long explanation is needed to show that in these few words the Psalmist sums up the bitter experiences and sorrows which we, at least of the older generation, have suffered from our youth at the hands of the gentile populations surrounding us.

"As impressions of early life take deep hold, and as in my later years I still had no cause to modify these impressions, it is no wonder that I came to think that Christ himself was the plague and curse of the Jews—the cause of our sorrows and persecutions.

"In this conviction I grew to manhood, and still cherishing it I became old. I knew no difference between true and nominal Christianity; of the fountainhead of Christianity itself, I knew nothing.

"Strangely enough, it was the horrible Tisza Eslar blood accusation which first drew me to read the New Testament. This trial brought from their lurking-places all our enemies, and once again, as in olden times, the cry re-echoed, 'Death to the Jew!' The frenzy was excessive, and among the ringleaders were many who used the name of Christ as a cloak to cover their abominable doings.

"These wicked practices of men wearing the name of Christ only to further their evil designs, aroused the indignation of some true Christians, notably Professor Franz Delitzsch of the Leipzig University, who, with pens on fire and warning voices, denounced the lying rage of the anti-Semites. In articles written by the latter in defence of the Jews, I often met with passages where Christ was spoken of as he who brings joy to man, the Prince of Peace, and the Redeemer; and his Gospel was extolled as a message of love and life to all people.

"I was surprised and scarcely trusted my eyes when I

found, in a hidden corner, the book which some thirty years before I had taken in anger from a Jewish teacher. I opened the book, turned over its pages and read. How can I express the impression which I received?

"Not the half had been told me of the greatness, power, and glory of this Book, formerly a sealed book to me. All seemed so new, and yet it did me good, like the sight of an old friend who has laid aside his dusty, travel-worn garments, and appears in festive attire, like a bridegroom in wedding robes or a bride adorned with her jewels."

For two or three years Rabbi Lichtenstein kept these convictions locked in his own breast. He began, however, to preach strange and new ideas in his synagogue, which both interested and astonished his hearers. At last he could contain himself no longer. Preaching one Saturday from the "Parable of the whited sepulchre," he openly admitted that his subject was taken from the New Testament, and he spoke of Jesus as the Messiah, the Redeemer of Israel.

He embodied his ideas in three publications, appearing in rapid succession, which created a sensation among Jews, not only in Hungary, but throughout the continent of Europe. And no wonder! For here was an old and respected Rabbi, still in office, calling upon his people to range themselves under the banner of Jesus of Nazareth, and hail him as their true Messiah.

As was inevitable, as soon as official Jewry realized the significance of Rabbi Lichtenstein's position, a storm of persecution broke loose upon him. And he, who but a few weeks before was classed among their noblest of leaders and teachers, was now described as a disgrace and a reproach.

The charge was made that he had sold himself to missionaries. Some even asserted that he had never written the pamphlets himself, but had only been bribed to sign his name to them. He was cited to appear before the assembled Rabbinate in Budapest. He obeyed. On entering the hall he was greeted with the cry, "Retract! Retract!"

"Gentlemen," he replied, "I shall most willingly retract if you can convince me that I am wrong."

Chief Rabbi Kohn proposed a compromise: Rabbi Lichtenstein might believe whatever he liked, if he would only refrain from preaching Christ. And as to those dreadful pamphlets which he had already written, the mischief could be undone by a very simple process: the Conference of Rabbis would draw up a document to the effect that Rabbi Lichtenstein wrote what he did in a fit of temporary insanity!

Rabbi Lichtenstein answered calmly but indignantly that this was a strange proposal to make, seeing that he had only now come to his right mind. They then demanded that he resign his position as Rabbi and be formally baptized. He replied that he had no intention of joining any church; that he had found in the New Testament the *true Judaism;* and that he would remain as before, with his congregation.

He did so, and this in spite of many persecutions and reproaches which were heaped upon him. From his official position as District Rabbi he continued to teach and preach from the New Testament. This was a touching testimony to the strong attachment of his own community, which alone had the power to make request for his dismissal. As a matter of fact, much pressure was brought to bear, and some members of the congregation and relatives of his wife were completely ruined by loss of trade, but still they clung to him.

By this time Rabbi Lichtenstein and his writings had become widely known, and various church and missionary organizations sought his services. The Papacy, too, learned of the existence and significance of the man, and a special emissary from the Pope visited Tapio Szele with tempting offers if the Rabbi would enter the service of Rome.

To all he had one reply: "I will remain among my own people. I love Jesus my Messiah; I believe in the New Testament; but I am not drawn to join Christendom. Just as the prophet Jeremiah, after the destruction of Jerusalem, chose rather to remain and lament among the ruins of the

Holy City with the remnant of his brethren, so will I remain among my own brethren as a watchman from within, to warn them and to plead with them to behold in Jesus the true glory of Israel."

At last, however, with his health much impaired by the many trials and sorrows which fell to his lot, he voluntarily resigned his office as District Rabbi. He settled in Budapest where he found ample scope for his talents, but opposition to him was relentless.

He was shadowed and even physically attacked on the street. His barber was bribed to disfigure his beautiful beard. His landlord kept a close watch on everyone who visited him, and reported to the rabbinical authorities. But, as a stream stemmed in its course forces for itself new channels, so he was continually interviewed and drawn into discussion with Jews from every walk of life.

"Wisdom cries without and causes her voice to be heard in the street," he wrote to his friend in London, David Baron. "Doctors, professors and officials come to my house. Many families of position also visit us and condemn the harsh conduct of the Rabbinate here in relation to me. I often have grave and important discussions with Talmudists and Rabbis who wish to bring me to a compromise, and it is worthy of note that many who formerly had no knowledge of the New Testament have afterwards asked me for a copy."

For over twenty years Rabbi Lichtenstein witnessed in many parts of the Continent to the truth as he saw it in Christ. At last the storms of controversy, misunderstanding and antagonism began to tell on him. His spirit, however, remained undaunted.

About this time he wrote: "Dear Jewish brethren: I have been young, and now am old. I have attained the age of eighty years, which the Psalmist speaks of as the utmost period of human life on earth. When others my age are reaping with joy the fruits of their labors, I am alone, almost forsaken, because I have lifted up my voice in warning: 'Return, O

Israel, return unto the Lord thy God; for thou hast stumbled in thine iniquity. Take with you words, and return unto the Lord' (*Hosea* 14:2-3).

"I, an honored Rabbi for nearly forty years, am now in my old age treated by my friends as one possessed by an evil spirit, and by my enemies as an outcast. I am become the butt of mockers who point the finger at me. But while I live I will stand on my watchtower, though I may stand there alone. I will listen to the words of God, and look for the time when he will return to Zion in mercy, and Israel shall fill the world with his joyous cry: 'Hosannah to the Son of David! Blessed is he that cometh in the name of the Lord! Hosanna in the highest!' "

Quite unexpectedly he was taken ill and lingered only a short time. As he realized that his end was approaching, he said, in the presence of his wife and the nurse:

"Give my warmest thanks and greetings to my brethren and friends; good night, my children; good night, my enemies, you can injure me no more. We have one God and one Father of us all who are called children in heaven and on earth, and one Messiah Jesus who gave his life for the salvation of men. Into thy hands I commend my spirit."

The day was dismal; it was eight o'clock in the morning of Friday, October 16, 1909, when the aged Rabbi entered into the presence of his Lord.

How different was his beautiful spirit of love and forgiveness from the bitter spirit of his enemies! On the day after his burial there appeared an editorial in the ALLGEMEINE JÜDISCHE ZEITUNG, the organ of the Jewish Orthodox party in Budapest, and it is here reproduced to show the relentless hatred and persecution which a Jewish Christian, however blameless his life, has to endure for having the courage of his convictions and for speaking out for the truth as he sees it.

Of course, the editorial contains many falsehoods and slanders, and was another attempt to discredit Rabbi Lichtenstein's testimony in the eyes of Jewry. Yet in its way it bears witness to the unique character of the man who, in his official capacity, proclaimed the basic doctrines of Christianity.

‏* (טאר צײנעס מיסםיאנארס.)
‏נעסטערן וואורדע הייֵ דעֵ עהעמאליַזע עגז־
‏לאֵנע ראבבינער פאָן מאפעיַגֵ־סעלע אי־
‏ליככמענשטײן ימ״ש בעערדיגט. שאָן אלם
‏ראבבינער שטאנד עֵ אים דיענסטע דעֵ זעע־
‏לענסאַנֵגערישען מיססיאָן. אויף דעֵ ידישען קאָג־
‏צעל פֿאֵרקינדעטע עֵ גרונד־לעהדרען דעם כרי־
‏סטענטהומס אונד עֵ נאב אײנע בראשירע הער־
‏אוים, אין וועלבעֵ עֵ דיא יודען צור אנערקעג־
‏נונג דעם נירתדעֵים דעֵ כריסטליכען רעליגיאָן
‏אויפֿ֑אֵֵדערטע. ערסט נאכרעם דעֵ שקאנדאל
‏שאָן לאנגע נעדויערט האטטע, בעוואַג דאם פע־
‏סטעֵ נעמאָלאַגע ־אבבינאט דיא נעטיֵנדערענֵ־א־
‏ וענטאאַנץ צו מאפיֵַ־סעלע, דיא ציטײסט אײם
‏אַ‏סערווואנדמען ליכטענשטײַ׳ם בעשטאאֵַד, אידם
‏אײנע אבפֿאֵרטיגונג צו נעבען, דאטיט עֵ־ יעֵ
‏ראבבינעֵ־שטעללע ענטואַג.ע. זיטהעֵ לעבטע
‏ריעזעֵ ,זקן מטֵה׳ אין בדראַסעסס פֿאן דעם
‏פעלרע, וועלבעם אידם דיא ענגלישע מיספיאַ:ם.
‏פעזעללשאַפֿ֑ט נאב, ווייל עֵ זיינען נאמען צו
‏מיספיאַ:ם־צוויעקקען אויסבעריטען ליעסם. פֿאֵ־טעלל
‏נעטײַפֿ֑ט האט עֵ זיך אבעֵ ניבט, אינֵ זאַ
‏וואורדֵע דיעזעֵ ,מסֵ׳ת וסדיח׳ אויף דעם פֵ־יֵעֵ־
‏האֵ֑ץ דעֵ פעםטעֵ־ נעאָלאַנען חיק בעֵ־אבעֵן.
‏שם רשעים ירקב!

A literal translation of the Yiddish editorial reads as follows:

DEATH OF A MISSIONARY

"Yesterday the former Reform Rabbi of Tapio Szele, I. Lichtenstein—may his name be blotted out!—was buried here. While still rabbi he was in the service of the soul-entrapping mission. From the Jewish pulpit he proclaimed the foundation doctrines of Christianity, and wrote a pamphlet in which he invited Jews to recognize the Founder of the Christian religion. Not until the scandal had lasted quite a while did the Reform Rabbinate of Budapest succeed in inducing the representatives of the community of Tapio Szele, composed for the most part of relatives or friends of Lichtenstein, to demand his dismissal, in order that he should withdraw from the Rabbinate.

"Since that time the old apostate has lived in Budapest on money supplied him by English missionary societies, because he lent his name to missionary purposes. He was not, however, formally baptized, and thus this 'deceiver and misleader' was buried in the cemetery of the Reform Synagogue of Budapest. 'The name of the wicked shall rot.'"

The editor of the ALLGEMEINE JÜDISCHE ZEITUNG may be assured that, though "the name of the wicked" and of all liars and slanderers shall indeed be "blotted out" and "rot," the name of Rabbi Isaac Lichtenstein shall be recorded among the heroes of the Spirit.

"*I Am Not Alone*"

By JOHN COURNOS

John Cournos was born into an Orthodox Jewish home in Czarist Russia. As a child he had much to suffer from ignorant gentiles who called him "Christ killer." The impressions of childhood left an indelible mark on his mind. Since so-called Christians hated Jews, Cournos in turn hated Christ.

He was a mature man and had made a name for himself in literature, having some six novels to his credit, besides several plays, a volume of poetry, a biography, and many short stories, when he took up the reading of the New Testament. To his amazement he found that the Christianity of Russia had little in common with the teachings of Jesus. The Christians of Russia hated Jews, and Jesus was not only a Jew, but he stressed love towards fellowman, regardless of race.

We quote from Cournos' book, AN OPEN LETTER TO JEWS AND CHRISTIANS:

— ◆ —

"There is a fundamental, dignified reason for the Jewish reclamation of Jesus. A very simple, very honest reason. And that is that Jesus was a Jew—the best of Jews.

"That Jesus was essentially and even quintessentially a Jew, must not for an instant be lost sight of. Jesus was not only a Jew. He was the apex and acme of Jewish teaching, which began with Moses and ran the entire evolving gamut of kings, teachers, prophets, and rabbis—David and Isaiah and Daniel and Hillel—until their pith and essence crystalized in this greatest of all Jews.

"For a Jew, therefore, to forget that Jesus was a Jew, and to deny him, is to forget and deny all the Jewish teaching that was before Jesus; it is to reject the Jewish heritage, to betray what was best in Israel.

"To be a true Jew is to be a true Christian. To be a true Christian is to recognize the Jewishness of Christianity. The fate of Judaism and Christianity hangs together.

"As demonstrated by history, it is the tragedy of life that simple truths are rarely understood, or, if understood, disregarded. And yet we need not despair. Truth, if it be truth, always and inevitably leaves behind some residue of itself. Against the darkness of the world, a rallying cry is necessary, the stimulus of an ennobling and revivifying idea. We Jews and Christians alike must answer the challenge with a counter-challenge—the struggle of Jesus to establish a free spiritual kingdom on earth founded on mercy and love.

"It took me fifty years to arrive at this idea, taking into consideration the fact that I began at its other end, and in direct opposition to it, and that my experience has not been primarily a bookish one. Things rooted in childhood have deep roots, to be measured by the years they have been nourished.

"It may seem an even greater wonder that now, after a lapse of nearly fifty years, I should feel the strongest compulsion to step boldly out into the open and affirm with a deep conviction which has been slowly and inevitably growing upon me—until silence is out of the question—that the time has come, is indeed ripe, for us Jews to reclaim Jesus and to reinterpret him.

"I am not alone, however, in arriving at the inevitable conclusion . . . I know a number of Jews who believe as I do, who believe that it is time that we Jews reclaimed Jesus, and that it is desirable that we should do so. Some of them hesitate to speak, lest their own people disclaim them.

"A great Jewish novelist said to me a year or two ago: 'We Jews should come to terms with Christianity.' These persons, it will be said, are intellectuals and do not represent Jewry. I reject this notion, because, to take three examples among them: one is a novelist whose books are about Jews and read by Jews; one is an educator whose work is among Jews and who knows Jews exceptionally well; and one is a scholar interested in Jewish Sunday schools. If he were permitted by the elders he would include among his readings of 'gems' of Jewish literature, the Sermon on the Mount.

"Our rabbis should frankly and openly affirm that Christ is our own, our very own, flesh of our flesh, and bone of our bone, and he came not 'to destroy the Law or the prophets . . . but to fulfill.' He is our prophet, our greatest prophet, the keystone of our ultimate faith."

A Lamed-Vovnik

By HENRY EINSPRUCH

Hayim Yedidiah Pollak was one of the most remarkable men I have ever known. Born in 1854 in a little village near Stanislau, Galicia, his father intended him to become a rabbi, but, being left an orphan in childhood, he was reared by a relative.

Pollak enjoyed excellent educational advantages. He attended the University of Berlin, as well as Abraham Geiger's HOCHSCHULE, an academy for Jewish studies, and, before he reached the age of twenty-two, had received the degree of doctor of philosophy. He was a thorough Hebrew and Greek scholar; read Latin and French; spoke Polish, German, Yiddish and English with ease. In his old age he mastered the Holland Dutch language to such an extent that he could preach and also write in it for the press. His linguistic versatility was little short of phenomenal. If he was not literally able to speak all languages it was only because he had never had occasion to use them all! He was also learned in most departments of knowledge: history, philosophy, theology, and literature.

While pursuing his studies Pollak became acquainted with the New Testament. He was struck by the pure Jewish character of the evangelist Matthew, and also felt himself attracted by the mysticism of John. In the course of his studies at Geiger's HOCHSCHULE, he discussed these things with one of his teachers, Israel Levi. There was a heated discussion between them with the result that Pollak was dismissed from

הָעֵדוּת.

(עֵדוּת לְיִשְׂרָאֵל)

עדות־התורה והתעודה, על כל סגלות ישראל ויהודה

ספר עתי

נכון לכלי חפץ, ערוך מִזְמָן וקבוע, לשומרי תורת משה ועדות ישוע,
יוֹ״ל

לפי חוברות, במספר מסֻמָּנות, ולא לפי חדשים ועתים מזֻמָּנות,

מאת

הישראלי איש־המשיח, ידידי׳, בן אהרן׳ המצליח.

ספר רביעי	Ch. Th. Lucky. הַמְעוֹרֵךְ.	חוברת ראשונה

אנשים אחים, שמעו נא !

(דבר אל אחב״י המאמינים בישוע).

אנשים אחים, זה היום תחלת מעשי לחדש מלאכת העדות
אחרי אשר היתה נחבאה אל הכלים זה ארבע שנים, ואמרתי
אל לבי, טרם אני נגש אל המלאכה אדברה נא אליכם, אחי
המאמינים מבית ישראל, דבר בראשונה. — הן אנשים אחים
אנחנו, כמוכם כמוני מצור יהודה חוצבנו, בני יעקב אנחנו, ילדי
ישורון כולנו. כטובכם כמוני תלמידי המשיח אנחנו, כי נפקחו
עינינו, אחרי אשר הקשקשים נפלו מהן ונמצא את אשר עליו
נבאו משה וכל הנביאים. אחים אנחנו, גם אם לא כל דרכי
כדרכיכם ולא כל דעותי כדעותיכם. גם אם משמאילים מאוד
אתם לפי דעתי, עוד משפט וצדקה לנו לקרא "אח" איש אל
רעהו, כי כולנו בני אומה אחת, וכולנו חוסים בצל ישוע אנחנו,
אשר בו כולנו אחד (אל הגלטיים ג׳ : כ״ח) לכן שאוני נא אם
כמצות שאול, שליח אדונינו, אעשה והוכח אוכיח אתכם היום.
הנה שאול, השליח הגדול, צונו להוכיח כאה את כל המתרפה
במעשי הטוב (השני׳ אל התסלוניקים ג׳ : ט״ו), להזהיר ולהוכיח
איש את עמיתו יום יום, למען לא נפול במוקשי מרמת החטא
(אל העברים ג׳ : י״ג), להתבונן איש אל עמיתו לעורר איש את
אחיו לאהבה ולמעשים טובים, ולהוכיח זה את זה בראותנו כי
קרוב היום, אחרי אשר לנו דרך חדשה, דרך חיים, דרך אשר

the school. Israel Levi is quoted as predicting, "Nothing good will come out of Pollak, and in the end he will be a most *unlucky* man."

Pollak never forgot that Levi had called him an "unlucky" man, and after he accepted Jesus as his Messiah, he changed his name from Hayim Yedidiah Pollak to Ch. Theophilus Lucky — lucky, the fortunate one.

After completing his studies at the University of Berlin, he came to America and entered Union Theological Seminary in New York. On the voyage from London he met a man who had lost his coat. Lucky gave him eight dollars to buy a new one, which left him bankrupt in a strange land. This incident illustrates his characteristic generosity.

Upon graduation from Seminary with honors, Lucky was ordained to the Gospel ministry, and was associated with the Seventh Day Baptist Church. He felt the weight of the responsibility which lay upon his shoulders to carry the message of the Messiah to his brethren, but preferred to follow the method of St. Paul, which was to urge Jews to accept Jesus as Savior, and then allow them to observe their honored customs if they so desired.

Lucky had an ardent love for Israel and a deep regard for the Laws of his fathers. He believed that a Jewish Christian should not forsake the holy Sabbath, the observance of the Jewish festivals, and the dietary laws. His diet was strictly kosher.

On Friday evenings he would always attend synagogue and heartily join in all the prayers. On *Yom Kippur*, the Day of Atonement, Lucky stayed in the synagogue all day and fasted. He also observed *Tisha B'ab*, the day on which the Temple was destroyed.

Lucky began the publication of a Hebrew paper entitled, EDUTH l'YISRAEL, "The Witness for Israel," mainly for educated Jews. His writings were in the purest Biblical and post-Biblical Hebrew, and his own thoughts were expressed with elegance, copiousness and perspicuity. The renowed

Hebrew scholar, Professor Franz Delitzsch, praised his knowledge of the Hebrew language and the genuine Christian spirit which permeated his writings. Some of his articles seemed to be suffused with a soul-enkindling spirituality. In everything he wrote, Christ was all.

There was scarcely a country in Europe where Lucky had not been. He labored in his native Galicia, as well as in Russia, Roumania, Servia, Germany, England, and Holland. He was acquainted with leading people in these countries, and had an extraordinary memory. His friends were his friends in a very personal way, and included Hebrew scholars and other Jews of note throughout Europe and America. Numbered among them were the late Dr. Solomon Schechter, the giant of Jewish scholars, down to many an obscure rabbi.

I first heard of Lucky in 1911 when I came upon his Hebrew journal, EDUTH l'YISRAEL. The make-up of the paper greatly intrigued me, and a letter to the editor resulted in correspondence between us, which I still have among my prized possessions. I finally went to Stanislau and met Lucky face to face.

I shall never forget my meeting with him. He was intensely human and a brilliant conversationalist. While he was modest, he was not cringing or fawning. He had shapely hands, long artist's fingers, scrupulous personal cleanliness and neatness. His gentle eyes, high forehead and silvery white beard, together with his instinctive refinement and aristocratic bearing and presence, made an impression on me which I shall never forget.

Lucky was a man of simple life and utterly unselfish. He was a devoted follower of Christ, a man of gracious spirit, understood by few, loved by many. Scholars consulted him as an expert in Hebraica, and commanded his enthusiastic attention.

He was a true and loyal son of Abraham. In early life he had committed to memory the Old Testament in Hebrew. A friend opened the Hebrew Old Testament to one of the prophets and challenged him, but Lucky said, "Start it for me." After a few words, he continued the chapter and repeated it to the end.

A cricital Jewish writer, Samuel Freuder, makes the following comment: "Lucky was a Jewish missionary and an honest man; a strange creature indeed . . . Yet, as the Talmud has it, 'A myrtle among weeds remains a myrtle.' Lucky was absolutely truthful and honest . . . The townspeople did not look upon him with the usual feeling of hatred shown an apostate. Love begets love, and they knew how intense was his love for the Jewish people."

Professor M. Weisberg, author of THE HISTORY OF NEO-HEBREW LITERATURE, who knew Lucky personally for fifteen years, refers to him as "a most interesting personality, and an idealist whom both Jews and Christians respected and loved. His manner of life was like that of a *Lamed-vovnik*" (one of the thirty-six righteous men to whose piety, according to Jewish tradition, the world owes its continued existence).

Lucky died in 1916, at the age of sixty-two, and was buried in the Jewish cemetery at Plau, in Mecklenburg. To the many who knew him, his name will long be a fragrant benediction.

A Jewish Bishop

in China

By HELEN ALPERT LEVIN

Only rarely does one happen upon the names of William Carey, Adonirom Judson, David Livingstone, or even Albert Schweitzer. The results of their deeds go marching on, but their memory is limited to certain groups or religious circles.

Of even rarer memory is one Samuel Isaac Joseph Schereschewsky, the Lithuanian Jew, who labored in Shanghai with stupendous zeal, although with a paralyzed body, to make the Bible available to some 400,000,000 Chinese.

The excellence of his translations from the Hebrew and Greek into the Mandarin dialect and the "Easy Wenli" have made them the basis and model of all later versions, and have resulted in enthusiastic eulogies of Schereschewsky's skill, persistence, and knowledge.

Max Müller, philologist of Oxford University, has classed Schereschewsky as one of the six most learned Orientalists in the world.

Schereschewsky's early days seem to have been like those of other Jewish boys of his time, except for a precocity in Hebrew. He was born in 1831 in Lithuania, in the small town of Tauroggen. His parents had determined to make of him a rabbi. They died soon, however, and Schereschewsky lived with a relative, a timber merchant in good circumstances.

BISHOP SCHERESCHEWSKY IN HIS STUDY

He was unhappy, and left at the age of fifteen to wander and starve over Russian Poland and Germany. He attended the Rabbinical Seminary in Krazi, the town neighboring Tauroggen, where he studied the Talmud and Mishnah in Hebrew and Aramaic. So proficient did he become that at the age of seventeen he tutored in a Russian Jewish family, and at the age of eighteen wrote poetry in Hebrew.

After Krazi he moved to another town, Zhitomir, where he entered another Seminary for rabbis, more profound discussions of Talmudic problems, brightened by considerably finer hair-splitting.

At this time Schereschewsky was as identical in thought as he was in appearance to the hundreds of other Jewish boys who were roaming over Europe, searching out knowledge, and gravitating towards towns containing a substantial Jewish population. They wore long black coats, round hats, and earlocks. Life was a gloomy affair of not enough sun and too much abstraction. They chanted long prayers or followed the intricate reasonings of the more brilliant rabbis. And they hungered often. When Schereschewsky was a student in Frankfort his daily rations were a loaf of bread divided into three portions for the three meals.

Rather suddenly came a change in his thoughts. The story is that a fellow student smuggled a copy of the New Testament in a Hebrew translation into the Rabbinical School at Zhitomir. Not finding it of interest, he passed it on to Schereschewsky who, after careful study, became convinced that in Jesus the messianic prophecies of the Old Testament and the age-long hopes of his people had been fulfilled. The conviction rested, however, until after Schereschewsky had won honors as a student at the University of Breslau and had determined to sail for the United States. He stopped in Hamburg on the way. There he met a Christian Jew by the name of Jacobi, who befriended him and gave him letters of introduction to friends in the United States.

One of Jacobi's letters was addressed to the Rev. John

Neander, also a Christian Jew. Neander introduced numerous others and, when the Christian Jews of New York planned to observe the Passover together, Schereschewsky was included as a guest. At the end of the ceremony, each one rose and told what faith in Christ meant to him. Schereschewsky was deeply stirred, and at last he rose and said, "I can no longer deny my Lord. I will follow him."

He was about twenty-nine years old when he was graduated from the General Theological Seminary of the Episcopal Church. He declined a professorship in the Seminary, explaining, "I want to go to China to translate the Bible." His friends intimated that he was sailing to what would be the graveyard of his talents, but Schereschewsky prepared to leave and became one of a group who left New York for Shanghai on the clipper ship *Golden Rule*. During the long voyage they applied themselves diligently to the study of Chinese, but no one's progress was as swift as that of Schereschewsky's. Soon he far outstripped his companions, and on landing astonished the native teachers by his ability to write good classical Chinese.

Shanghai offered the best facilities for studying languages, and there Schereschewsky remained for two years. The following year he began the series of scriptural translations into Chinese for the more than one-fourth of the world's population. The series officially began with the translation of portions of the Psalms into the Shanghai colloquial.

Schereschewsky then moved on to Peking in order to perfect himself in the Mandarin dialect, the general language of the Chinese people. One historian claims that his command of the three Chinese languages, Shanghai colloquial, Mandarin, and the literary Wenli, was so marked that he was employed as interpreter by the American Ambassador to China at the time.

In Peking, in collaboration with the English Bishop of Hongkong, Dr. Burdon, he translated the Book of Common Prayer into Mandarin. It took them a year, and at its completion was the first Mandarin version of the Prayer Book that had ever been made.

Next came an even more important achievement — the translation of the Old Testament into Mandarin, on which Schereschewsky worked with a committee of Chinese scholars. Some years later he wrote: "The Old Testament has chiefly been assigned to me, owing to my familiarity with Hebrew. I am told that I ought to regard it as my special call in this country until this work is done. Being a Jew by birth, and having enjoyed in my earlier years a good Jewish education, I know Hebrew better than any other language. As to my knowledge of Chinese, I hope I possess the average knowledge of it."

Schereschewsky's next achievement added climax and drama to his previous ones and put him in the front rank of Orientalists and translators. He set about translating the New Testament into Mandarin, a task which took four years, during which time he preached every Sunday to large crowds in Shanghai and outside the west gate. His version of the New Testament has never been rivaled for its scholarship.

After sixteen years in China, Schereschewsky left on furlough for the United States. He was elected to the Bishopric of Shanghai, and received an honorary Doctor of Divinity degree from Kenyon College and Columbia University. Just before his return to Shanghai he campaigned vigorously and successfully for funds with which to establish a college where modern science and Christianity would be taught along with the Chinese classics. St. John's University in Shanghai was the result.

Several years later Bishop Schereschewsky undertook the translation of the Prayer Book into Easy Wenli, the literary or book language which was understood by all Chinese who could read, no matter what their local dialect might be.

The following summer was a fateful one. While super-vising the building of a church in Wuchang, Schereschewsky suffered a severe sunstroke from which he never fully recovered.

It left him with a disease of the spine which paralyzed his body. However, the vigor of his mind was untouched.

He finally returned to the United States, and resumed the work of translation, but since he could not write or secure a Chinese scribe, he purchased a typewriter, the "Caligraph." He soon discovered that he could type with one finger—the middle finger of his right hand. When his finger failed him, he would grasp a small stick in his fist and punch the keys with it.

Schereschewsky began on the revision of the Mandarin Old Testament, hammering out on the typewriter with his one finger the English equivalents of the Chinese characters. At first he worked five or six hours a day, then seven, then eight, sometimes nine. In a little more than a year the revision of the Mandarin Old Testament was completed. Then he went on to a new translation of the entire Bible into the Easy Wenli, a work which took him six years. His industry and patience were infinite and incredible. The American Bible Society suggested that he go to Japan to supervise its publication, which he did, taking up residence in Tokyo until the book was published.

We are indebted to Dr. James A. Muller, author of the "Apostle of China," for the following description of Schereschewsky. "He was five feet nine inches in height, weighed about a hundred and fifty pounds, and was of spare physique. He had perfect teeth and never went to a dentist in his life, except to have them cleaned. He had a clear olive complexion, brilliant dark grey eyes, and black hair and beard, which became silver-white in later years. He seldom slept more than six hours. He was quick-tempered, and impatient with stupidity. Faulty reasoning, foolish questions, and failure to use one's brains made him angry. But he was equally quick to make amends when he lost his temper. He had immense powers of concentration. While at work he could be diverted by nothing. He was particular to a degree about his personal appearance. He was a fiend on punctuality.

Always prompt himself, he expected promptness from others.''

Schereschewsky's life has been catalogued as one of the romances of Bible translation. But such a phrase is as deceptive as it is fluent. His life contained too much pain and toil to beg for so pleasant a label. For the last twenty-five years of his life he was almost completely paralyzed, but with indomitable perseverence he continued his remarkable series of Bible translations. "I am never without pain,'' he once confessed to a colleague.

For forty years Schereschewsky devoted himself almost exclusively to Bible translation, and the list of his accomplishments is long.

His death at the age of seventy-five, on October 15, 1906, brought to an end the career of the one-time rabbinical student of Tauroggen.

Sir Leon Levison—
The Lion Hearted

By NAHUM LEVISON

In the ancient, holy city of Safed, sacred to Jewish tradition, a boy, Leon Levison, was born. He was the fourth son of the distinguished Rabbi Nahum Levison, who was famous as a profound expositor of the principles of Jewish Law and customs.

Rabbi Levison wanted his sons to have the best Jewish education available, so he invited Rabbi Joshua of Acre, one of the most famous teachers of youth in the Holy Land, to come to Safed as tutor. Rabbi Joshua was a saintly and unworldly man, a strict observer of Rabbinic Law. It has been said that he was one of a small group who kept silence from Friday afternoon till Saturday evening, discussing nothing except things concerning the Sabbath.

Rabbi Joshua became very fond of Leon, and Leon idolized him and was much impressed with his kindly and beautiful spirit. But Leon felt that the study of the Torah by itself was not a sufficient occupation in life. For had he not been told that Rabbi Hillel was a woodcutter; Rabbi Shammai a carpenter; and many other celebrated rabbis were shoemakers, tailors, sandalmakers, smiths, potters! Leon, too, wanted to work with his hands, and was finally given permission to study tailoring. He was very proud of his work and persisted

Sᴉʀ Lᴇᴏɴ Lᴇᴠɪsᴏɴ

until he was able to make a suit for himself. That accomplished, tailoring was given up for an interest in agriculture. Leon experimented with cross grafting, and developed a particularly luscious eating grape, superior to any grown in the Holy Land.

At the age of thirteen he made his *bar mitzvah*, became a son of the Law, and was now responsible for his own actions in the moral law. He had no patience with any law that did not have love, mercy, and forgiveness at its root, and early began to show great concern in other people's problems.

The story is told that he was barely fourteen when a quarrel arose between two sheikhs which could easily have led to the beginning of a blood feud. It was a dangerous situation, and as a rule Jews kept out of quarrels between Arabs. But Leon, accompanied by a Jewish courier named Herschel, met with each sheikh and arranged an offer of peace, which was accepted.

Leon seems to have been a born leader. The young Jews of Safed were divided among the sephardic (Spanish-Portuguese) and Ashkenazi (German-Polish-Russian). These young men had formerly very little to do with each other, and Leon welded them into a group which rendered considerable service to the community.

His determination to become efficient in the things that interested him led him to study French. His argument was, "You must know what other people think." It was this same determination that ultimately brought him into contact with Christianity. He wanted to learn English, but the only teachers available were those connected with the School of the Free Church of Scotland Mission. In spite of his great prejudice, Leon and a few of his friends arranged to study secretly at night with Masud-el-Hadad, a Christian teacher in the school. English lessons continued, and the discussions also included the claims of Jesus as Messiah.

After the first winter, the teacher invited the medical missionary, Dr. George Wilson, to speak to the young Jewish men. Dr. Wilson was a man of kindly disposition, and before long his visits to the class became frequent and the youths took a great liking to him. He was a strong witness for Christ, and a number of the young men, including Leon, showed more than passing interest.

Dr. Wilson suggested that Leon go to Scotland to visit his uncle, Dr. Hood Wilson, pastor of the Barclay Church, Edinburgh. Here Leon worked for two years in a factory to earn his living. He took classes at the University and also studied at New College, all with the idea of fitting himself for Christian work.

Leon's parents loved him very much, and it was difficult for him to break the news to them of his acceptance of Christ. The worst of it was that they thought he was now an enemy of the Jewish people. He returned home, and on the way said, "I would let them curse me, beat me, do what they like to me for believing in Christ, but I cannot have them think that I hate our people, that I do not love them with all my heart."

The meeting with his mother showed the deep affection that bound them to each other, but also her terrible anger at his acceptance of Christ.

"You must leave the Nazarene out of this house; you must not mention his name so long as you are in this house. Do you hear?"

"Yes, mother," was Leon's reply, "but I cannot leave him out. He and I are inseparable."

She kissed him, and nothing further was said. The next day was Saturday, and Leon went to synagogue with members of his family. He promised a donation to help the poor, and stayed till the prayers were over. He was criticized by some who thought that he had compromised his faith, but Leon never flinched.

"If you want me to explain, I will do it. If you care to condemn me without hearing me, I have a clear conscience before God and my Messiah."

For over thirty years Leon worked in Scotland for the

Jews and for Christ. He was fascinated by the Zionist movement, and never relinquished his dream of a Hebrew Christian colony in the Holy Land. He was a man of strong, but gracious personality, of infinite resource, wise statesman-ship, broad human sympathies, and consecrated Christian spirit. He worked along his own lines, and his efforts were most effective when, in the privacy of his home, he met many of his brethren who came to him secretly by night to inquire about the Messiah.

On the public platform and in the pulpit, Leon was also supreme. He went throughout the length and breadth of Scotland, arousing the conscience of Christians to a sympathetic understanding of the Jew. His rare natural gift for forming friendships, readily obtained openings for him to advocate the cause of better understanding between Jews and Christians, and as an eloquent speaker he won the interest and support of his audiences.

During World War I, Leon raised over £200,000 for various Jewish Relief Funds, and also did invaluable secret service work for the British Government. Honors poured in upon him. He was knighted by the King, made a knight of the Holy Sepulchre, and was presented with the Freedom of the City of Edinburgh.

Sir Leon was the author of a number of books, including a "Life of Paul"; was director and chairman of the publishing house of Marshall, Morgan & Scott; and one of the founders and first president of the International Hebrew Christian Alliance. As president he was no mere figurehead, but threw himself, heart and soul, into the work.

The needy were his brothers and sisters; the fallen his care; and his greatest gift that of enlisting the sympathy of others in good causes. He was roused to indignation where others were concerned, and once he had taken up the cause of an individual, or an ideal, he fought for it with all the courage of his name, "Lion."

To the end, Sir Leon remained essentially humble,

simple-hearted, a devout lover of the Messiah whom he served so well, and at heart the boy who once wandered over the Galilean hills and found in their silence the peace of God first revealed there two thousand years before, in His own Son, born a Jew.

His work for Jews in Russia, Germany, Poland, central Europe, the Holy Land and America will never be forgotten. He was universally respected and, in the country of his adoption, was honored by all people, from the highest to the lowest.

Upon his death, tributes poured in from the great, the near-great, and the humble, but one expression seems to sum them up: "A Prince has fallen in Israel. In very truth, there has never been such a man in this generation."

Would I? Would You?

One day in loved Jerusalem
There rushed a shrieking, maddened crowd
Upon a lowly kneeling form,
Before his God and Savior bowed,
And when with cruel stones they crushed
His beautiful and gentle life,
He prayed the Father to forgive
Their ignorance and raging strife.
   This man was Stephen. Lo! a Jew,
   Who died for Christ.
   Would I? Would you?

See! far upon a lonely isle,
An aged man with snowy locks,
Exiled to labor in the mines,
His only temple wind-swept rocks.
Ah! Once he leaned on Jesus' breast
And gazed with fond adoring eyes
Into that face where love divine
Still beams upon us from the skies.
   This man was John beloved, a Jew,
   Witness for Christ.
   Am I? Are you?

A Galilean fisher stood
Amid a fierce and angry throng,
No tremor spoke of hidden fear,
His face was peaceful, calm and strong,
And when they nailed him to a cross,
As they had nailed his blessed Lord,
He gloried thus to die for Christ
And counted it a rich reward.
    This man was Peter. Lo! a Jew,
    Who died for Christ.
    Would I? Would you?

A captive bound was brought one day
To Nero's judgment seat at Rome;
For Christ he wore the heavy chain,
For Christ he had no wealth nor home;
The noblest martyr Rome could boast
Of all the thousands that she slew,
The great apostle sent by God
To Gentiles with the message true.
    This man was Paul. E'en Paul, the Jew,
    Who died for Christ.
    Would I? Would you?

ACKNOWLEDGMENTS

"I Am Not Alone" from *"An Open Letter to Jews and Christians"* by John Cournos. Reprinted by permission of Oxford University Press.

Some of the material in this book has appeared in previous publications. We give credit to *Raisins and Almonds* and *When Jews Face Christ*.

OTHER PUBLICATIONS

The New Testament in Yiddish

Raisins and Almonds

The Good News According to Matthew

The Man with the Book